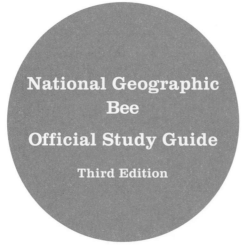

National Geographic Bee

Official Study Guide

Third Edition

by

Stephen F. Cunha

NATIONAL GEOGRAPHIC

Washington, D.C.

In memory of John Joseph Ferguson and Ann Judge, *who perished aboard American Airlines Flight 77, which crashed into the Pentagon on September 11, 2001. They were traveling to California with six Washington, D.C., teachers and students as part of an educational field trip sponsored by the National Geographic Society. Joe and Ann were tireless, visionary supporters of the Society's education outreach programs. Their enduring work directly benefits countless teachers and students throughout North America.* —SFC

For information about special discounts for bulk purchases, please contact National Geographic Books Special Sales: ngspecsales@ngs.org

For rights or permissions inquiries, please contact National Geographic Books Subsidiary Rights: ngbookrights@ngs.org

Cover design by David M. Seager

The text type is set in New Caledonia; headlines are set in Clarendon.

All questions and place-names were accurate and current at the date of their actual use in the National Geographic Bee.

Library of Congress Cataloging-in-Publication Data
Cunha, Stephen F.
  National Geographic Bee official study guide / by Stephen F. Cunha.
    v. cm.
Includes index.
Contents: The why of where: defining geography—Bee basics: understanding the contest—Top ten study tips—Conquering the questions—Tips from bee finalists—Resources Genghis Khan would have loved.
  ISBN 0-7922-7850-X (paperback), 2002 edition
  ISBN 0-7922-7983-2 (paperback), 2005 edition
  ISBN 0-7922-7997-2 (library), 2005 edition
  ISBN 978-1-4263-0198-8 (paperback), 2008 edition
1. National Geographic Bee—Juvenile literature.
2. Geography—Competitions—United States—Juvenile literature. 3. School contests—United States—Juvenile literature. [1. National Geographic Bee. 2. Geography—Competitions. 3. Contests.] I. Title.
  G74 .C86 2002
  910'.79'73—dc21
                        2002003423

Printed in the United States of America
10/CML-RRDC/2

Contents

Caitlin Snaring

Foreword

"A city that is divided by a river of the same name was the imperial capital of Vietnam for more than a century. Name this city, which is still an important cultural center," was my final question in the National Geographic Bee. My winning answer was "Hue" (Hway). When studying, I had read about Hue, the former capital of Vietnam and the home of the emperors of the Nguyen dynasty in the 19th to mid-20th centuries, but I never knew that this single fact would crown me a champion and begin a new chapter in the story of my life.

During the next few days, I appeared in the national news on NBC, CNN, and CBS, and on local Seattle TV stations. Also, I was interviewed by Matt Lauer and Meredith Vieira on the *Today* show and by several other radio shows, newspapers, and magazines. Much was made about the fact that in the Bee's 19-year-history, I was only the second girl to be named National Champion. When I returned to Redmond, I had the privilege of meeting the Washington State Governor, received a congratulatory letter from

President Bush, and was honored by our state senator, who placed me in the Congressional Record. I was even invited to throw the opening pitch for a Seattle Mariner baseball game!

Geography comes from the Greek words "geo," meaning "the earth," and "graphy," meaning "to describe," so it means "to describe the earth." It is the study of places on Earth and of Earth's effect on how we live. It is everything from mountains to mineral resources, from lakes to languages, and from rivers to religions. But there is more. Geography is also understanding how our lives affect the planet so that we can help protect it. By helping us understand such things as cultural patterns, events in the news, and economic situations, geography promotes an understanding of countries, places, and people around the world.

If you think geography is fascinating or you are interested in knowing a little more about the world around you, I encourage you to test your geography wits in the Bee. The Geographic Bee is an awesome experience. It offers the possibility to win some money, a little fame, and new friends—the kind who share your interest in geography. Even if you don't end up becoming a national champion, I guarantee that what you learn by studying for and competing in the Geographic Bee will benefit you for the rest of your life, plus it will give you a better understanding of our wonderful, majestic world!

Caitlin Snaring
Champion
2007 National Geographic Bee

*I like Geography best,
he said, because your
mountains and rivers
know the secret. Pay no
attention to boundaries.*
—BRIAN ANDREAS,
AMERICAN POET

Introduction

This book will help you prepare for the National Geographic Bee. It is written to answer the most common question that students, teachers, and parents ask of Bee officials: "What's the best way to study for the Bee?" The comprehensive nature of geography makes it hard to offer an easy answer. Most academic contests in spelling and math provide a word or problem list that makes preparation easier. Although you can pinpoint some aspects of the Bee, a good showing requires understanding the nature of geography. In essence, you must learn the fundamental geographic patterns that will help you to think geographically. This book provides you with a framework for learning how to conquer this immense and fascinating subject.

The first chapter explores the world of geography and explains why it is so important to study the subject. Then the origin and purpose of the Bee as well as the structure and format of the contest are discussed. Chapter 3 provides tips on how and what to study for the Bee. Chapter 4 tells you how to look for clues in the questions and use the study tips to come up with the correct answers, then provides lots of real Bee questions so you can test yourself. Bee winners offer advice and inspiration in Chapter 5, and resources that will help you study are evaluated in Chapter 6. The Note to Teachers discusses various initiatives and support groups available for teaching geography more effectively and helping students prepare for the Bee.

Although we live at the dawn of the digital age, Thomas Jefferson's ideal regarding the truly educated person still stands:

> In the elementary schools will be taught reading, writing, common arithmetic, and general notions of geography. In the district colleges, ancient and modern languages, geography fully, a higher degree of numerical arithmetic...and the elementary principles of navigation.
> —Thomas Jefferson to M. Correa da Serra (1817)

Jefferson believed that a balanced curriculum produced more capable and enlightened citizens than one that focused on just one or two subjects. Although Jefferson never booted up a computer to surf the Web or e-mail his friends, he correctly forecast the value of exercising all parts of the human brain. Were he alive today, he would be pleased by your interest in geography and in the world around you.

What kind of young people enter the Bee? The Society's staff and those of us who work with them have about 20 years of data on this very subject. We find that Bee kids play instruments and compete in sports. Many run for student government and join school clubs. Some tour the globe with their parents; others journey mostly in their imaginations. Some kids say their favorite subject is math; others say literature, physical education, or even—gasp—geography. There are tall and short kids, big and small kids, funny kids, and very, very serious kids. Bee kids hail from our largest cities and smallest towns (the first national champion attended a one-room schoolhouse in rural Kansas). Some attend public or private schools; others are homeschooled. What unites them is a natural curiosity about our world.

This book can help you be more competitive at every level of the contest. But advancing through the rounds should not be the only reason to enter the Bee or to study these chapters. The real benefit comes from learning what geography is all about, and that alone will enrich your life forever. You'll be amazed how geography makes you a better reader, a more knowledgeable historian, a better mathematician, and a more versatile scientist. Geography links other subjects into a seamless whole whose sum greatly exceeds its parts. Most important, studying geography will help you become a more sensitive and aware citizen of our global community.

Let the adventure begin!

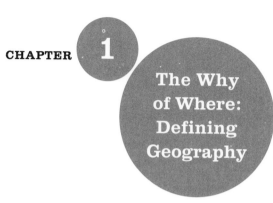

CHAPTER **1**

The Why
of Where:
Defining
Geography

From space I saw Earth—
indescribably beautiful
with the scars of national
boundaries gone.
—ASTRONAUT MUHAMMAD
  AHMAD FARIS, SYRIA (1988)

Imagine captaining a 17th-century merchant ship with a crew of 200 and a cargo hold stuffed with exotic goods from the Far East. You are London-bound to exchange your booty for gold coins and more shipping contracts from anxious merchants. Gazing across the Indian Ocean at sunrise, you take stock of the possible hazards that threaten success: pirates, sudden storms, rocky coastlines, and even mutiny. But the biggest danger of all is veering off course into an endless sea because you cannot plot your location accurately on the map.

Before John Harrison developed a special clock called the marine chronometer in the mid-1700s, sailors could not pinpoint their longitude—their location east or west of the prime meridian. Captains routinely lost hundreds of men and tons of cargo to starvation and storms while searching for a place to land. In Dava Sobel's wonderful book Longitude, *the author describes a dozen disasters,* including that of Admiral Sir Clowdisley Shovell. The admiral lost four of his five warships and 2,000 troops in 1707 after misjudging his longitude in the Scilly Isles, off the southwestern tip of England. Adrift in dense fog, the ships "pricked themselves on rocks and went down like stones." Yikes!

Fortunately, Harrison's ingenious clock enabled navigators to determine longitude by comparing the time of day on board ship with noon in Greenwich, England, which was (and still is) located on the prime meridian (0° longitude). Because latitude—the distance north or south of the Equator—was easy to calculate by observing the stars, sailors could now see where their latitude and longitude intersected on the map and determine their exact geographic location in an open ocean where there are no landmarks. (You'll learn more about latitude and longitude in Chapter 3.)

Early continental explorers also suffered when they lacked geographical information. Poor Hannibal crossed the Alps in the wrong time of year and nearly froze to death. Lewis and Clark almost perished in the mountains of Idaho and Montana because they didn't know how vast the Rocky Mountains were. And what were those Vikings thinking when they attempted to grow barley in Iceland a thousand years ago?

Knowing where places are located is an important first step to learning geography and enjoying the Bee. Fortunately for us, using maps and finding latitude and longitude are much easier today than during poor Sir Clowdisley Shovell's lifetime.

However, geography is much more than places on a map. In the words of Alexander Graham Bell, one of the founders of the

National Geographic Society, geography is "the world and all that is in it." Place-names such as Brazil, Stockholm, Mount Everest, and Yangtze River are to geography what the alphabet is to reading. They open the gate for boundless and lifelong learning. Knowing where places are on a map is important, but the real heart of geography is understanding why people settle in a particular place, who their neighbors are, how they make a living, why they dress and speak the way they do, and what they do for fun. Developing this sense of place will raise a flat map to life.

Geographers investigate our global climate, landforms, economies, political systems, human cultures, and migration patterns. They are concerned not just with where something is located, but also with why it is there and how it relates to other things. A good geographer knows how to combine this information from many different sources and how to identify patterns that can help us understand our complex world. Geography explains why your grandmother moved to Tucson (warm and dry climate), how oil from Kuwait reaches Italy (by way of the Suez Canal), where tropical rain forests grow (near the Equator), who faces toward Mecca as they pray (Muslims), and which continent is the most populated (Asia). In a nutshell, geography is the "Why of Where" science that blends and enriches history, literature, mathematics, and science.

Although place-names of the world are now thoroughly mapped and available in atlases, maps, books, and even online, knowing where you are and the geographic characteristics of that place are just as important today as in earlier times.

Understanding people and environments influences the location of everything from Wal-Marts to hospitals to software manufacturing plants. City planners need population projections and environmental data before they can approve plans to build housing developments, office buildings, and shopping centers. Engineers must study water resources and the lay of the land before starting any project (even a small hill or creek can greatly increase construction costs). Imagine trying to advertise a new product without knowing the composition (Hispanic, African American, Asian, European), age structure (teenagers or grandparents), and economic characteristics (farmers, factory workers, or professionals) of the people you want to buy it. Highway construction cannot proceed until facts about climate, soil, vegetation, and the number of people who will drive the proposed route are considered. Each day, kids everywhere awake in sheets of woven Egyptian cotton, pull on clothes stitched in Bangladesh, wolf down bananas grown in Central America, and grab schoolbooks printed in Singapore to board buses assembled in Michigan from parts made in Japan and Germany.

For more than a decade, the growth of our global society—the rising dependence of nations upon each other for trade and security—has made geographical studies more important than ever. Acronyms and abbreviations, such as NAFTA, GATT, EU, and WTO, are heard on the evening news. Schools from Alaska to Zambia stress second-language and culture studies to better prepare their students not just for a global economy but also for a more crowded planet where migration, tourism, and the Internet connect our global family more each day. The global war on terrorism further underscores the great importance of more fully understanding the people of the world, how they live, what they believe, and the environment and resources we share.

Whether you are the secretary of state for the United States or the secretary of your class, knowing geography will help you understand the world.

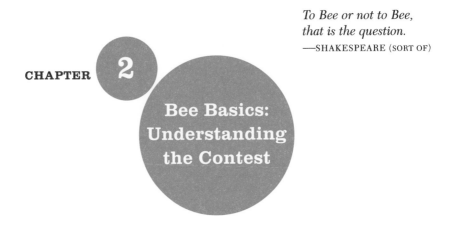

To Bee or not to Bee,
that is the question.
—SHAKESPEARE (SORT OF)

CHAPTER **2**

Bee Basics: Understanding the Contest

This chapter marches through the annual Bee calendar from registration to the national finals. It explains who is eligible to participate and the format at the school, state, and national levels. (It is important to note that although the Bee provides an instruction booklet to each registered school, the booklet contains recommended procedures only. Schools sometimes have to make adjustments to fit their needs.) Understanding how the Bee works and following the advice at the end of the chapter will help you relax, have fun, and perform better.

REGISTRATION

Registering is easy. Although only principals may register their schools, students (or their parents) can often stir teachers and principals into action. Check with school officials or go online to the registration link on our website to see if your school is entered for the upcoming Bee. If you are a middle school student who rotates among classes, the social studies teacher is your best bet, followed by the principal. Schools must register *each* year by the deadline (usually October 15). More information on Bee registration appears on page 121, or check for any extensions on our Web site: www.nationalgeographic.com/geographicbee.

ELIGIBILITY

All U.S. schools with any of the grades four through eight may register for the Bee. Students enrolled in a conventional public or private school may not compete as part of a homeschool Bee. Homeschooling associations may register to have a Bee for homeschoolers in their area. A student may compete in a magnet school Bee only if enrolled full-time at the magnet school. (A student enrolled part-time at a magnet school may not compete in the magnet school Bee.) Parents and teachers must pay close attention to these details to prevent a disqualification.

Students in grades four through eight who are not over the age of 15 by the time of the national finals may participate. The Bee is an open contest that does not separate students into age or grade-level categories. There must be a minimum of six student participants in a school to hold a school-level competition.

SCHOOL-LEVEL BEES

In mid November, the Society mails Bee packets to each registered school. The packet contains the suggested procedures, the question booklet, a medal for the winner, and a Certificate of Participation for each student who takes part. School officials then select the days for their Bee, so long as the competition falls within the dates established by the Society—normally anytime between mid-November and mid-January.

School Bees are the responsibility of the schools. Their decisions are final. These Bees are usually broken into a Preliminary Competition, which normally takes place in individual classrooms, and the Final Competition, which is often held in the school assembly room (cafeteria, auditorium, gym, etc.).

Preliminary Competition

These rounds usually require an oral response. A teacher or other moderator reads the questions aloud. You will be asked one question per round and will have 15 seconds to answer each question. To keep the contest moving, you are allowed to ask to have a question repeated or a word spelled only two times during the Preliminary Competition. Such a request to the moderator must be made immediately.

Once the question has been repeated or the word spelled, you will have the remainder of your 15 seconds to answer the question. You must start to give your answer before the 15-second time limit is up. If you do not answer within the allotted time, the moderator will say, "Time," give the correct answer, and move on to the next student. One point is awarded for each correct response; a pass is counted as an incorrect response. There is no penalty for mispronunciations (or misspellings, in the event of a written response) so long as the moderator can determine you know the correct answer. The student with the most correct answers wins the chance to advance to the Final Round.

Tiebreakers

If there are ties in determining the finalists, school officials will use a series of Preliminary Competition Tiebreaker Questions. Everyone involved begins with a clean slate—no hits and no misses. Students get the same question and write their answers on the paper provided. Again, there is no penalty for misspellings so long as the moderator can determine that the correct answer has been given. Questioning continues until the tie or ties have been broken.

Final Competition

The Final Competition consists of a Final Round and a Championship Round. If you are lucky enough to advance to this level, you may find yourself on a stage in the school auditorium. As with any contest or game, the pressure builds as you progress up the ladder. Expect some bright lights and audience noise, ranging from restrained gasps to thunderous applause.

In addition to the round-robin oral questions you encountered in the Preliminary Competition, the Final Round includes questions that require written responses (students are simultaneously asked the same question and respond by writing their answers on the paper provided). Other questions may involve graphs, maps, or photographs. If so, you will be given a copy of the visual to study up close before answering the question. But the biggest difference between the Preliminary Competition and the Final Round is that students are eliminated after giving their second incorrect answer. Once the third-place winner has been determined, the remaining two students advance to the Championship Round.

Championship Round

In the Championship Round the two contestants start with a clean slate. Both are asked the same questions simultaneously and given 15 seconds to write their answers. The moderator then asks the students for their answers. The student with the most correct answers wins the school Bee. Tiebreaker questions may be necessary to determine the winner. The champion receives a prize and certificate from the National Geographic Society, and every student who entered the school Bee receives a Certificate of Participation.

QUALIFYING TEST

To advance to the state Bee as a representative of his or her school, the school winner must take the written Qualifying Test. This test should be given in a quiet location in the school building. It must be monitored by a teacher who is not a parent or guardian of the school Bee winner. There are about 70 multiple-choice questions, covering the entire range of geographic inquiry, including a set that pertains to a map, table, or graph. There is a time limit of one hour. When time is up, the teacher administering the test must sign the certification statement on the answer sheet and mail it to the National Geographic Society. The test must be received by the Society no later than January 31 of the year of the test. Tests received after that date will not be graded. Faxes are not accepted.

The National Geographic Society scores one Qualifying Test from each participating school. The top 100 students (more if there are ties) from each of the 50 states, the District of Columbia, the Department of Defense Dependents Schools, the Atlantic, and the Pacific territories compete in the State Bees. The National Geographic Society appoints state Bee coordinators to coordinate this portion of the contest. In early March, Society officials notify the teachers of the students who qualify for the state competition.

STATE-LEVEL BEES

The state Bees are usually held in early April. An adult must accompany each student to the State Bee. In most cases this is a teacher, parent, or legal guardian. Other adults may substitute with school approval. Expect the Bee to begin with an opening assembly jam-packed with all 100 state finalists, officials, teachers, and a zillion family members. The room is abuzz with excitement and nervous anticipation.

The contestants break into five groups of 20 students. The seating and room assignments are determined by random drawing before the Bee. Just as in the school-level competition, there are preliminary, final, and championship rounds (and tiebreakers if necessary). The Final and Championship Rounds are held in front of a large audience and are very exciting. In general, the public is not allowed to attend. Once the pressure is off, you will impress yourself with how many questions you can answer correctly! The same procedure that is recommended to schools for determining the school-level winners is used to determine the

THE NATIONAL-LEVEL BEE

State Bee winners meet at the headquarters of the National Geographic Society, in Washington, D.C., in late May to compete for the title of national champion. The national-level format is similar to that of the previous levels of the Bee except that the questions are harder and there are more rounds involving visuals, such as photographs, maps, and graphs. Also, in the Final and Championship Rounds you have only 12 seconds to answer each question. The top ten winners of the Preliminary Competition compete in the Final Round. Alex Trebek, host of TV's *JEOPARDY!*, has moderated the Final and Championship Rounds since 1989. To see if these rounds are televised in your area, check the Bee Web site for broadcast information. It's always fun to follow along and see how many questions you can answer. The top three finishers take home college scholarships. The total prize and scholarship monies awarded at the school, state, and national levels make the Bee one of the richest academic competitions for schoolkids on Earth.

THE CANADIAN GEOGRAPHY CHALLENGE

The Canadian equivalent of the National Geographic Bee also features a series of competitions at the school, provincial or territorial, and national levels that are designed to test students' knowledge and skills in geography.

Currently there are two grade levels to the Challenge: Level 1 for grades four to six and Level 2 for grades seven and above. All Level 2 competitors must be under the age of 16 as of June 30 (the end of the school year in which the Challenge takes place). Only schools, not individuals, may register for the Challenge, and any number of students or classes within a school may compete. All registered schools receive an instruction booklet, a question and answer booklet, and prizes. The kits are available in English and French.

The competition for Level 1 students ends at the school level; Level 2 students with the top 50 scores on the written qualifying test in each province or territory are invited to a Provincial or Territorial Challenge, usually held in April. The highest-scoring students from this competition compete in the National Final in May. The top three scorers are declared the Canadian National Champions and receive scholarships.

BEE GREAT: ADVICE TO CONTESTANTS

The following list is the result of more than a decade of "Bee-ing" with students, teachers, and parents. Although my experience has been mostly at the state level, these tips will help at any level in almost any type of competition. They are included here to help make the Bee a truly memorable and fun event.

Relax! Cramming hurts your brain

The evening before and the morning of the Bee are prime times to relax, play with your dog, and bike ride with a sibling or friend. Don't stay up the night before conversing with owls while attempting to cram in a few last-minute facts. This contest is fun, so rest up and dream of faraway lands.

Set aside part of each day to prepare for the Bee. Remember that geography is an integrative subject that takes time to learn and appreciate. Avoid flipping flash cards on the way to the Bee. (Several times I have seen parents quizzing students just moments before the Bee!) This adds tension that can detract from the quality of your performance and your enjoyment of the competition.

Healthy body, healthy mind

Whether you live in Paris, Pyongyang, or Philadelphia, the best advice is to stay fit, eat a balanced diet, and avoid spending so much time hunting for facts online or looking things up in books that your physical fitness declines. A healthy body houses a sharper and more capable mind.

Many students at every level of the Bee find that eating before the contest is a difficult idea to stomach. Yet your brain is a big muscle, and to keep it working at full throttle requires high-octane fuel. That is to say, CHOW DOWN BEFORE THE BEE! Don't arrive hungry. An empty stomach will make any jitters you have feel much worse. This problem does not affect every student, but if you know that big events—however much fun they may be—make it difficult to eat, then here is some food for thought.

First, eat a well-balanced dinner the night before the Bee. This way, unless your stomach is the size of a thimble, you'll have calories in your tank at least through noon the following day. Second, eat at least a small breakfast that includes some juice and something solid, such as fruit, carbohydrates (toast, muffins, cereal), or eggs. Try to avoid greasy and high-fat foods, as they are harder to digest and can make your tummy do back flips.

Dress for success

Although this is a special event, you don't need to rent a tux or a frilly evening gown. Even ties and dresses are rare. Most kids— both girls and boys—pull on something comfortable. Pants or a skirt with a clean shirt or blouse are a good choice. Of course, you'll want to look neat. Remember that advancing to the finals at any level could land you onstage.

Take a deep breath

It's easy to panic when you hear a question that freaks you out! "Oh no, I can't remember the largest city on Mars!" Forgetting to breathe or taking several gasps is a natural reaction. If this occurs during the Bee, relax, take a deep breath, collect your thoughts, and then look for clues in the question that will help you figure out the correct answer. Remember, you have 15 seconds (except in the national finals) to answer each question. Believe it or not, that's a long time! Failing to take in oxygen will make it more difficult to think and will increase that feeling of alarm!

Listen to every question in each round

When competing in the oral rounds, listen to every question and every answer. You may pick up clues that will help you come up with the right answer when it's your turn.

Stand by your first answer

Unless you are certain of an error, stick with the first answer that comes to mind. Believe it or not, studies show that students who change their answers or get stuck trying to choose between two answers usually select a less accurate choice the second time.

Ignore your friends

While you're competing, don't look at people you know, especially just before and during your turn. Ask your friends, teacher, parents, and other family members to make themselves invisible by sitting as far away as possible. Also, tell them to photograph you *after* the Bee, not while you are trying to remember which country borders Zimbabwe on the east. (Mozambique, of course!)

Speak loudly and write with a big stick

Make your answers known in very decisive ways. Speak in a loud, clear voice. When a written answer is required, write clearly in LARGE, BOLD LETTERS. The teacher/moderator must be able to understand your answer and read your handwriting.

Remember: It is impossible to fail in the Bee. Just by taking part you are already a success!

CHAPTER **3**

Top Ten Study Tips

*All the rivers
run into the sea;
yet the sea is not full;
Unto the place
from whence
the rivers come,
thither they return
again.*
—ECCLESIASTES

The ten trusty tips outlined in this chapter will help you "Bee" ready. This powerful advice has been assembled over many years from students just like you. A small army of teachers added their two cents' worth, too.

Don't expect to learn everything about geography in just one school year. Remember that you are eligible to enter the Bee from the fourth through the eighth grade. No one expects a fourth grader to know as much as an eighth grader, but it's not impossible. Susannah Batko-Yovino was only a sixth grader when she became the national champion in 1990! By participating each year, you will increase your knowledge of geography and self-confidence. These ten study tips will teach you the basics and how to build on them to recognize geographic patterns. You'll be thinking like a geographer in no time!

Choose Your Tools

Getting started in geography is easy if you have the right tools. Spending a part of each day with these tools will expand your world in a hurry. A few pointers on using these are presented here. You'll find advice about specific products and where to find them in Chapter 6.

A large **WORLD MAP** should be in every home. Concentrate first on learning the continents, oceans, and largest islands. Then focus on countries, capital cities, and major physical features (such as mountain ranges, lakes, and rivers), gradually adding other places and features to your vocabulary. Hang your world map next to your bed or on the closet door. Put smaller maps of each continent around your house. Position one in the bathroom so you can learn the countries of Africa while brushing your teeth. Laminated map place mats let you explore Italy while slurping spaghetti. You can also tape maps behind the front seat of your family car and visit South America on the way to school.

A good **ATLAS** is the next essential tool. These come in all sizes, with many excellent and reasonably priced volumes to match your skill level. Be sure to use one that is less than five years old so that it includes important name updates.

Look for three other features when choosing an atlas. First, it should have both physical maps (emphasizing natural features) and political maps (emphasizing country boundaries and cities). Second, make sure it includes an index (or gazetteer) that alphabetically lists place-names that appear on the maps. This will help you find unfamiliar locations. Finally, look for text that includes information about each continent, country, and world region (such as Southeast Asia or Middle America), plus a section on geographic comparisons (longest rivers, largest cities, etc.).

BLANK OUTLINE MAPS are the third item for your kit. These black-and-white line maps outline the continents and countries. Important physical features such as major rivers and mountain ranges may also appear. Use these to practice labeling countries, cities, rivers, lakes, mountains, islands, and other geographic information as you learn it. Always start with the most obvious features, then add more detailed information as you progress. Blank outline maps are a great way to quiz your growing knowledge of the world. Some online sources are listed in Chapter 6.

A **GEOGRAPHY REFERENCE BOOK** rounds out your tool kit. Although maps and atlases help you learn where Mongolia, Mauna Loa, and other places are located, a good geography reference book explains *why* they are located there, *who* lives there, *what* they do, and *how* the landscape came to be. These books usually arrange information in alphabetical order either by single topic (Agriculture, Alluvial Fan, Avalanche), or by category (Earth Science, Population, Wildlife). The most helpful ones enrich the text with numerous maps, photographs, charts and graphs, and a glossary of terms. A good reference book takes you to the next level of geographic learning by raising flat maps to life. This marks the point where memorization evolves into real geographic exploration and discovery!

TIP #2 Learn the Language of Maps

A good map is worth a thousand pictures. Expert map readers can absorb oceans of geographic information in a short time. But to understand all that a map can tell you, you must first learn the language of maps.

LATITUDE and **LONGITUDE** are the imaginary lines that divide Earth's surface into a grid. Under this system, both latitude and longitude are measured in terms of the 360 degrees of a circle. The latitude and longitude of a place are its **COORDINATES**. Coordinates mark the **ABSOLUTE LOCATION** of a place. Understanding coordinates, you can use a map to locate any point on Earth.

Latitude is the distance north or south of the **EQUATOR**, the line of 0° latitude that divides the Earth into two equal halves called hemispheres. The top half is the **NORTHERN HEMISPHERE**, and the bottom half is the **SOUTHERN HEMISPHERE**. Lines of latitude are also called **PARALLELS** because they circle the Earth without ever touching each other. From the Equator we measure latitude north and south to the Poles. The **NORTH POLE** is located at 90°N latitude, and the **SOUTH POLE** is located at 90°S latitude.

There are other important parallels that you should learn. The parallel of latitude $23\frac{1}{2}°$ north of the Equator is called the **TROPIC OF CANCER**, and the parallel $23\frac{1}{2}°$ south of the Equator is the **TROPIC OF CAPRICORN**. The region between these two parallels is called the **TROPICS**. The **SUBTROPICS** are the zones located between $23^{1/2}°$ and about 40° north and south of the Equator.

The parallel of latitude $66^{1/2}°$ north of the Equator is called the **ARCTIC CIRCLE**, and the parallel $66^{1/2}°$ south of the Equator is the **ANTARCTIC CIRCLE**. The region between $66^{1/2}°$N and 90°N is called the Arctic; the region between $66^{1/2}°$S and 90°S is called the Antarctic. Both regions can simply be called polar.

Longitude is the distance east or west of the **PRIME MERIDIAN**, the point of 0° longitude. This is also the starting place for measuring distance both east and west around the globe. Lines of longitude are called **MERIDIANS**. They also circle Earth, but connect with each other at the Poles.

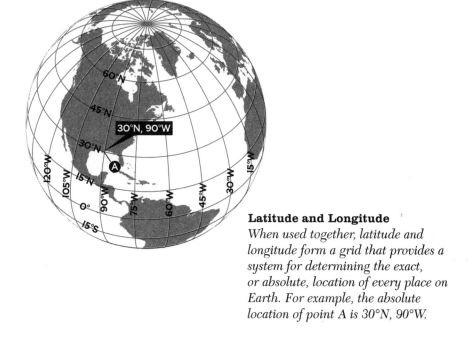

Latitude and Longitude
When used together, latitude and longitude form a grid that provides a system for determining the exact, or absolute, location of every place on Earth. For example, the absolute location of point A is 30°N, 90°W.

We also use the coordinate system to determine direction. When you face the North Pole (90°N), the sun rises to your right (east) and sets to your left (west). The south is behind you. These four points—north, south, east, and west—are **CARDINAL DIRECTIONS**. Any point *between* two cardinal directions is an **INTERMEDIATE DIRECTION**. For example, looking north and partly to the east is said to be looking northeast. But if you turn around and glance south and partly to the west, you are looking southwest.

A **GLOBE** is the only accurate representation of our spherical Earth. Think of a globe as a scale model of Earth with a paper or plastic map mounted on its spherical surface. Globes are great to study because unlike most flat maps, they show continents and oceans in their true proportions. Size, shape, distance, and direction are all accurately represented. Projecting this round shape onto a flat sheet of paper to make a map distorts these elements.

To solve the problem of distortion, mapmakers use a variety of **MAP PROJECTIONS** to portray our curved Earth on a flat sheet of paper. Each projection distorts Earth according to a mathematical calculation. Three commonly used projections are the Mercator, the Winkel Tripel, and the Goode's Interrupted Homolosine. The **MERCATOR** projection is helpful to navigators because it allows them to maintain a constant compass direction as they travel between two points, but it greatly exaggerates areas at higher latitudes. The **WINKEL TRIPEL** is a general purpose projection popularly used for political, physical, and thematic maps because it minimizes distortion of both size and shape. The

GOODE'S INTERRUPTED HOMOLOSINE minimizes distortion of scale and shape by interrupting the globe. This type of equal-area projection is useful for mapping comparisons of various kinds of data, such as rain forests and population density.

MERCATOR

WINKEL TRIPEL

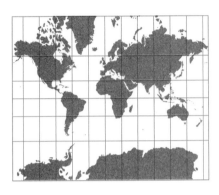

GOODE'S INTERRUPTED HOMOLOSINE

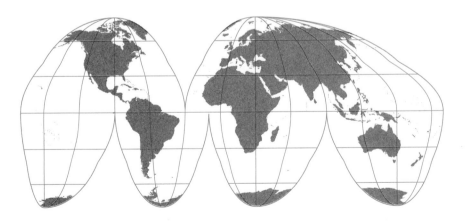

There are two main types of maps. **PHYSICAL MAPS** empha-size natural features such as mountains, rivers, lakes, deserts, and plains. Mapmakers often use shades of color to indicate different elevations. **POLITICAL MAPS** use lines to show boundaries between countries, points to show cities, and various other symbols to show roads, airports, canals, and other human-related features. Examples of these two kinds of maps are on the facing page.

We use latitude and longitude to determine the absolute loca-tion of physical and political features and **RELATIVE LOCATION** to explain the underlying reasons for that precise location and to show the interconnection of geographic phenomena.

For example, the geographic grid pinpoints Chicago's absolute location at 41°N latitude, 87°W longitude. However, the Windy City's location on the shore of Lake Michigan is *relative* to the his-toric water commerce routes favored by early Native Americans and settlers. Without Lake Michigan, Chicago might not exist.

Similarly, Khartoum, the capital city of Sudan, is located at 15°N latitude, 32°E longitude, *relative* to the confluence of the Blue and the White Nile. Without this confluence of rivers, this city out in the center of the Sahara would not have become such an important economic center.

Physical features are located relative to the geologic processes that created them. For example, Mount Rainier, in Washington State, is located at 47°N latitude, 122°W longitude, relative to the collision of two tectonic plates (moving slabs of Earth's crust) that created the Cascade Range. As a result, Mount Rainier shares the same geologic origin as the other volcanoes located north and

PHYSICAL MAP

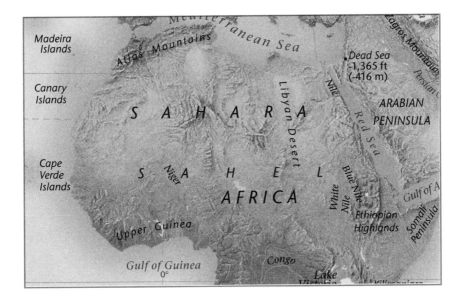

POLITICAL MAP

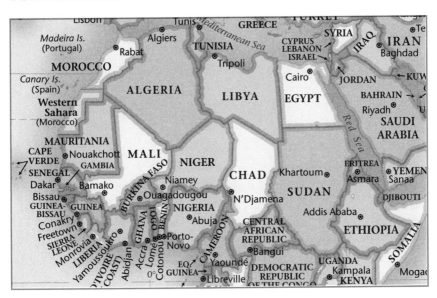

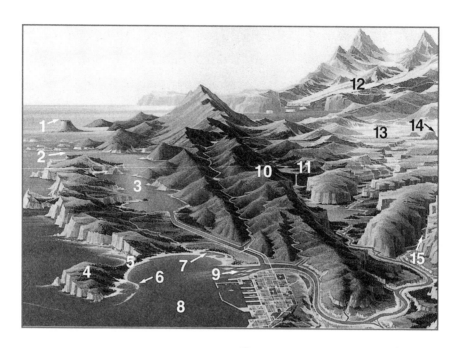

IMAGINARY LANDSCAPE

1 Volcano

2 Strait

3 Sound

4 Peninsula

5 Isthmus

6 Spit

7 Lagoon

8 Bay

9 Delta

10 Divide

11 Reservoir

12 Glacier

13 Desert

14 Mesa

15 Canyon

south of it. Without the tectonic plate boundary, this part of the Pacific Northwest would have a much different physical environment and human settlement pattern than we see today.

Use the world maps, atlases, and geographic reference books in your tool kit to learn more about these concepts and the language of maps. They are the building blocks for more learning and the source of many Bee questions.

The diagram of an imaginary landscape on the facing page was used in a round of questions in a state-level Bee to quiz students on their ability to identify physical features. Students were asked to give the number that best represented a specific physical feature. Of course, they didn't have the benefit of being able to see the answers! They are provided for you so that you can use this as a study tool for learning some very basic physical terms. You will find definitions for each of these terms in your geographical reference book. Learn them, and try to find examples of each on physical maps. You can be sure that geographic terms are a frequent topic for Bee questions.

TIP #3

Study the A "Bee" Cs

Once you know how to read maps, the next step is to learn the most important place-names that go on them. This memorization develops your global sense of place. Learning place-names is like learning your ABCs. Without knowing the alphabet, you can't spell words. Without knowing place-names, you can't identify places and features on a map or understand the interrelationships between physical and human activities. They are a necessary and important building block to greater geographic knowledge.

The number of place-names can be overwhelming. Organizing them into physical and political groups can be helpful. Start with the first categories in each group and work your way down. Don't just memorize a list of names and figures. Find each feature or place on the map and take time to learn about it and what it's near.

PHYSICAL FEATURES

THE CONTINENTS

	AREA (sq mi)	(sq km)	% of Earth's Land
Asia	17,208,300	44,570,000	30.0
Africa	11,608,000	30,065,000	20.2
North America	9,449,000	24,474,000	16.5
South America	6,880,000	17,819,000	12.0
Antarctica	5,100,000	13,209,000	8.9
Europe	3,841,400	9,947,000	6.7
Australia	2,968,000	7,687,000	5.2

THE OCEANS

	AREA (sq mi)	(sq km)	% of Earth's Water Area
Pacific	65,436,200	169,479,000	46.8
Atlantic	35,338,500	91,526,400	25.3
Indian	29,839,800	74,694,800	20.6
Arctic	5,390,000	13,960,100	3.9

Note: Although some geographers consider Europe and Asia as one continent called Eurasia, National Geographic counts them as two landmasses to make a total of seven continents. Likewise, some maps show a Southern Ocean around Antarctica. Others show this body of water as the continuation of the Atlantic, Pacific, and Indian Oceans. The tables at the bottom of the previous page list the names of the continents and oceans in order by size.

HIGHEST POINT ON EACH CONTINENT

	feet	meters
Everest, Asia	29,035	8,850
Aconcagua, S. America	22,834	6,960
McKinley (Denali), N. America	20,320	6,194
Kilimanjaro, Africa	19,340	5,895
El'brus, Europe	18,510	5,642
Vinson Massif, Antarctica	16,067	4,897
Kosciuszko, Australia	7,310	2,228

LOWEST POINT ON EACH CONTINENT

	feet	meters
Dead Sea, Asia	-1,365	-416
Lake Assal, Africa	-512	-156
Death Valley, N. America	-282	-86
Laguna del Carbón, S. America	-344	-105
Caspian Sea, Europe	-92	-28
Lake Eyre, Australia	-52	-16
Bentley Subglacial Trench, Antarctica	-8,383	-2,555

TEN LARGEST SEAS

	AREA (sq mi)	(sq km)
Coral	1,615,260	4,183,510
South China	1,388,570	3,596,390
Caribbean	1.094,330	2,834,290
Bering	972,810	2,519,580
Mediterranean	953,320	2,469,100
Sea of Okhotsk	627,490	1,625,190
Gulf of Mexico	591,430	1,531,810
Norwegian	550,300	1,425,280
Greenland	447,050	1,157,850
Sea of Japan (East Sea)	389,290	1,008,260

TEN LARGEST LAKES

	AREA (sq mi)	(sq km)
Caspian Sea, Europe-Asia	143,200	371,000
Superior, N. America	31,700	82,100
Victoria, Africa	26,800	69,500
Huron, N. America	23,000	59,600
Michigan, N. America	22,300	57,800
Tanganyika, Africa	12,600	32,600
Baikal, Asia	12,200	31,500
Great Bear, N. America	12,100	31,300
Malawi, Africa	11,200	28,900
Great Slave, N. America	11,000	28,600

TEN LARGEST ISLANDS

	AREA (sq mi)	(sq km)		AREA (sq mi)	(sq km)
Greenland	836,000	2,166,000	Sumatra	165,000	427,300
New Guinea	306,000	792,500	Honshu	87,800	227,400
Borneo	280,100	725,500	Great Britain	84,200	218,100
Madagascar	226,600	587,000	Victoria	83,900	217,300
Baffin	196,000	507,500	Ellesmere	75,800	196,200

LONGEST RIVERS*

	miles	kilometers
Nile, Africa	4,241	6,825
Amazon, S. America	4,000	6,437
Chang (Yangtze), Asia	3,964	6,380
Mississippi-Missouri, N. America	3,710	5,971
Murray-Darling, Australia	2,310	3,718
Volga, Europe	2,290	3,685

Antarctica has no flowing rivers

* These lists name the longest river and the major mountain range on each continent. Rivers are listed longest to shortest. Mountain ranges are listed in alphabetical order.

MAJOR MOUNTAIN RANGES*

Alps, Europe

Andes, South America

Atlas Mountains, Africa

Great Dividing Range, Australia

Himalaya, Asia

Rocky Mountains, North America

Transantarctic Mountains, Antarctica

Ural Mountains form much of the boundary between Europe and Asia

EARTH'S EXTREMES

Hottest Place: Dalol, Danakil Depression, Ethiopia; annual average temperature—93°F (34°C)

Coldest Place: Plateau Station, Antarctica; annual average temperature— -70.4°F (-56.7°C)

Wettest Place: Mawsynram, Assam, India; annual average rainfall—467 in (1,187 cm)

Driest Place: Atacama Desert, Chile; rainfall barely measurable

Highest Waterfall: Angel Falls, Venezuela; 3,212 ft (979 m)

Largest Desert: Sahara, Africa; 3,475,000 sq mi (9,000,000 sq km)

Largest Canyon: Grand Canyon, Colorado River, Arizona; 277 mi (446 km) long along the river; 600 ft (180 m) to 18 mi (29 km) wide; about 1.1mi (1.8 km) deep

Longest Reef: Great Barrier Reef, Australia; 1,429 mi (2,300 km)

Greatest Tides: Bay of Fundy, Nova Scotia, Canada—52 ft (16 m)

THE POLITICAL WORLD

Most atlases list countries with statistical information, such as area and population, so that you can make your own chart of the largest and smallest by area and by population. Although area figures seldom change (unless there is a boundary change), population figures do. Use Web sites listed in Chapter 6 to keep up-to-date.

The countries of North America: North America is made up of 23 independent countries. It includes Canada, the United States, Mexico, the countries of Central America, the islands of the West Indies, and Greenland.

The countries of South America: South America is made up of 12 independent countries and one French territory, French Guiana.

The countries of Europe: Russia is usually counted as one of Europe's 45 independent countries. Although most of its land is in Asia, most of its people and its capital city (Moscow) are west of the Ural Mountains in Europe.

The countries of Africa: Africa has 53 independent countries. Most people live along the Nile and south of the Sahara.

The countries of Asia: China is the largest country located entirely in Asia and also the most populous of Asia's 46 countries.

Australia, New Zealand, and Oceania: Australia is a continent and a country. Geographers often include it and New Zealand with the islands of the south and central Pacific and call this region Oceania. Australia is the largest and most populous of the 14 independent countries in this region.

Antarctica: This is the only continent that has no independent countries and no permanent population.

TIP

4 Master Mental Maps

Studying geographic shapes and place-names will eventually fix mental maps in your brain. You'll be able to picture not only where a place is, but what's near it, who lives there, and lots more. The ability to produce mental images of the world characterizes all Bee champions. This requires atlas and reference book use and a good understanding of map scale.

MAP SCALE makes it possible to figure out what distance on Earth's surface is represented by a given length on a map. Large-scale maps show a limited geographic area such as a neighborhood or city in great detail. The scale on such a map may be expressed as the ratio 1:1,500, meaning that every inch on the map equals 1,500 inches on the ground. (That's 125 feet or less than half a football field.) This allows the cartographer to include street names, parks, and creeks. A large-scale map of the United States wouldn't fit in your backpack. In fact, you'd need a dump truck!

Small-scale maps have much less detail but cover a greater geographical area, such as a state, mountain range, or continent. The scale here may read 1:5,000,000 (one inch equals five million inches on the ground—a very long crawl). This level of detail is the only way to cover a large area such as a continent or the world so that you can study it as a whole.

The next step is adding more physical and cultural depth to these mental maps. The following categories will get you started.

PHYSICAL FEATURES

Vegetation Zones, or Biomes: There are four main categories of vegetation zones: forest, grassland, desert, and tundra. Start with these, then expand your knowledge by learning about the different types of vegetation within these categories. Vegetation is closely linked to climate.

Climate Zones: Climate is the long-term average weather conditions of a place. Most climate maps show at least five different zones: tropical, dry, temperate, continental, and polar. As you build your knowledge, you will become familiar with subcategories, such as tropical wet and dry, arid and semiarid, marine west coast, and Mediterranean.

CULTURAL FEATURES

Population Density: Population density is the number of people living in each square mile or kilometer of a place. The population density of a country is calculated by dividing its population by its area. Asia is the most densely populated continent; Australia is the least densely populated continent (excluding Antarctica). Check out your maps, and see if you can figure out why!

Religion: All of the world's major religions—Christianity, Hinduism, Judaism, Buddhism, Islam—as well as Shinto, Taoism, and Confucianism originated in Asia. They spread around the world as people migrated to new areas.

Languages: There are thousands of languages, but there are only 12 major language families. Languages in the Indo-European family, which includes English, Russian, and German, are spoken over the widest geographic area. Mandarin Chinese is spoken by the most people. Can you figure out why?

ECONOMIC FEATURES

World Economy: Familiarize yourself with terms such as primary, secondary, tertiary, and quaternary, as well as developed and developing, industrialized and nonindustrialized.

Commerce: Learn the major crops, minerals, and products that countries on each continent produce and export. Then take note of major trade alliances, such as NAFTA (North American Free Trade Agreement), the EU (European Union), WTO (World Trade Organization), and OPEC (Organization of Petroleum Exporting Countries).

Transportation: Study maps, charts, and graphs to learn about major trade routes by land, sea, and air.

Filling in your mental maps will take some time, so be patient. Find a study method that works for you and then hop to it!

Build Your Knowledge

Conquering place-names prepares you to tackle the biggest and most rewarding challenge of preparing for the Bee: learning about the world's primary physical and cultural patterns. Understanding how the world functions as an interconnected and dynamic system is what geography is all about. Studying these patterns prepares you to combine and layer more complex geographic information onto your basic mental maps. This takes time, but the rewards are great. The following suggestions are designed to help you reach this level.

COMBINE INFORMATION

Good geographers combine information from different sources to arrive at logical conclusions. They understand the basic patterns of climate, geology, vegetation, human settlement, migration, and commerce. Combining these patterns with a knowledge of regions and place-names will empower you to answer very specific questions that otherwise might have been a choice between two guesses. At the very least it will enable you to make an educated guess when you don't know the answer. The question analyses that follow explain how this works.

1. Which city recently suffered a severe earthquake, Tokyo or Omaha?
You may not recall any recent earthquakes, but you know that

Tokyo is in Japan, an island country off the east coast of Asia, along the tectonic Ring of Fire. Omaha is a city in Nebraska, a state located in the middle of the North American plate. Since more earthquakes occur around the rim of the Pacific Ocean than anywhere else, you correctly answer **Tokyo**.

2. Which is Germany's most important export crop, wheat or palm oil?
Using your mental maps, you know that Germany is a midlatitude country in western Europe. You also know that palm trees grow in warm tropical climates and that wheat grows in more temperate regions, like the American Midwest. Given Germany's location, you reason that it is more likely to have a temperate rather than a tropical climate, and you correctly answer **wheat**.

LEARN PATTERNS ON THE LAND

Interpreting a landscape is very different from memorizing names on a map. Geographers use **THEMATIC MAPS** to show patterns on the land. They start with a physical or a political base map and add layers of information to show whatever geographic theme they wish to emphasize—everything from world population and energy consumption (see map opposite, top) to shark attacks and local weather predictions.

CARTOGRAMS are special kinds of thematic maps. On them, the size of a country is based on a statistic other than land area. In the cartogram shown, population determines the size of each country. This is why Nigeria, Africa's most populous country, is shown much larger than Sudan, Africa's largest country in area.

THEMATIC MAP

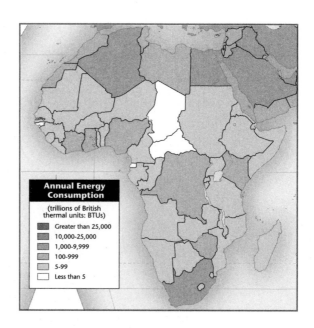

Annual Energy Consumption

(trillions of British thermal units: BTUs)

- Greater than 25,000
- 10,000-25,000
- 1,000-9,999
- 100-999
- 5-99
- Less than 5

CARTOGRAM

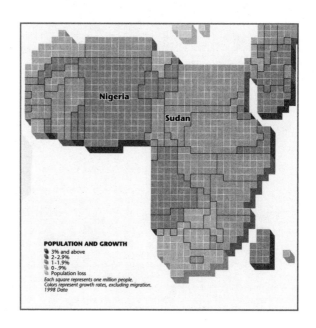

Nigeria

Sudan

POPULATION AND GROWTH

- 3% and above
- 2-2.9%
- 1-1.9%
- 0-.9%
- Population loss

Each square represents one million people.
Colors represent growth rates, excluding migration.
1998 Data

INTERPRETING GRAPHS

Graphs are another important tool that geographers use to convey information, and you can expect to encounter various kinds in the Bee. A special kind of bar graph called a population pyramid *(below, top)* shows the distribution of a country's population by sex and age. A more traditional style of bar graph shows water usage.

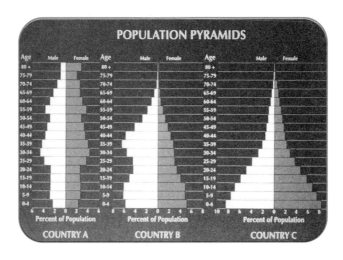

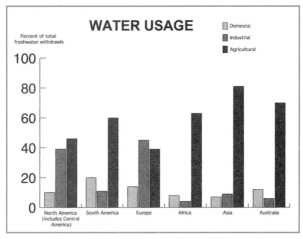

TIP #6 Make School Work for You

Geography is all around you! The first place to look is in school. History uniformly incorporates geography in discussing wars (the Russian winter froze the German Army in World War II), slavery (wind belts made the triangular trade possible), and ecological disasters (poor farming techniques and drought triggered the Dust Bowl during the 1930s). You will also find geography concepts in literature (Mark Twain, Robert Service, Laura Ingalls Wilder), science classes (especially Earth science and biology), mathematics (latitude and longitude, population studies, sun angles, etc.), and fine arts (dance, music, and paintings are all reflections of culture). You can even find geography in your school cafeteria (tacos, spaghetti, and rice). With good mental maps and the ability to combine information from different sources, you can spend your entire school day in excellent preparation for the Bee!

 ## Use Your Geographic Eyes

When you can think like a geographer and understand the major patterns that influence our physical environment, culture, and economy, it's time for some field observation. The following suggestions will get your nose out of the books and into the real world.

BECOME AN OBSERVANT MALL RAT

Stores are filled with goods from every corner of the world. The origin of these products and their movement around the globe tells us much about where raw materials such as wood, minerals, and cotton come from, who makes them into finished products such as furniture, baseball bats, and shirts, and who buys them. They also furnish clues about labor use, population growth rates, and the huge difference in wealth between rich and poor countries.

Combining information from product labels and packaging with your mental maps represents advanced geographic thinking. You can practice this in stores, at school, and at home by reading the labels and packaging on products to find out where the raw materials used to make them came from and who made them.

For example, many computers are manufactured in China from European and Japanese components. They carry a U.S.A. label and are packaged in boxes made in Mexico. Most toys are manufactured in China. Much of our clothing is stitched in Mexico, Central America, or Asia. Many books are printed in

Singapore. After much practice, you will find it easier to predict which country names will appear on boxes and labels. This is great evidence that your mental maps are becoming more detailed!

Check out stores that sell furniture (look for exotic woods), electronics (identify manufactured goods with components from multiple regions), and indigenous art (that comes from everywhere). A century ago, Americans prized goods made overseas for their exotic qualities. Today, it would be extraordinarily difficult to outfit a home with products made only in North America. Global connections are the heart of the world's economy.

STOMACH MORE GEOGRAPHY

Grocery stores offer products from everywhere. Look for New Zealand kiwis, Colombian coffee, Central Asian spices, Swiss chocolate, and Mexican avocados among the zillion other products from around the world that arrive in your local food store.

Be aware that geographic place-names incorporated into product labels can sometimes lead you astray. For instance, check out fine china from Ireland, India ink bottled in South America, chili peppers grown in Mexico, English muffins baked from Nebraska wheat, and Canadian bacon from hogs raised in Iowa!

ATTEND COMMUNITY AND LOCAL EVENTS

Local communities are a great geographic resource. Keep an eye out for free concerts and lectures. Visit your museums and library display cases. If you have a college or university nearby, watch for public lectures and exhibits.

Stay Current with Current Events

Current events questions query knowledge about natural disasters (Hurricane Katrina, fires in Greece, Andean earthquakes), cultural and political upheaval (Darfur, Myanmar, Israel and Palestine), international agreements (Kyoto Protocol, Ocean Treaty, Intellectual Piracy), and discoveries (archaeological finds, new plant species, energy, etc.). Almost any topic that is in the news, especially if it involves more than one of the categories mentioned above, is fair game for the Bee. Stories that have been the subject of recent Bee questions include the spread of AIDS, the Beijing Olympics, Iran's nuclear ambitions, and China's Three Gorges Dam.

For our purposes, we can divide current events into ongoing topics—such as global warming, immigration, and oil exploration—and breaking news stories, such as Noel Prize announcements, international border closures, and national elections.

Your local and regional media (newspapers, TV, radio) are great ways to keep tabs on our rapidly changing world. Online news sites are also good sources, and they report events from many different perspectives. You can scan online newspapers in a matter of minutes. They also offer great maps, photos, archived back issues, and links to related sites.

Read, Read, Read

Bee champions share a passion for reading. They read books, magazines, newspapers, cereal boxes, Web sites—anything they can lay their eyes on. They read at school, at grandma's, and on buses, trains, and airplanes. They read on weekends and throughout the summer. Reading helps build your mental maps of people and places around the world. At the same time, reading becomes more geographic once you have good mental maps that enliven and enrich almost any story or news item. You can add to your mental maps as you read by keeping a map handy. Use it to find new places and features and to understand relationships between the land and the people.

TIP #10 Play Games

Chapter 6 evaluates several games that use a quiz format like the Bee's to test your knowledge of geography. The Bee Web site offers geography questions to give you an idea of what the questions in the contest are like. You will find *GeoSpy, GeoBee Challenge,* and lots of other geography games at: http://kids.nationalgeographic.com/Games/GeographyGames

Playing these games offers several advantages. First, they simulate the Bee by asking questions from diverse topics that require an answer in a fixed amount of time. Second, they can help you identify your weak areas so that you can concentrate on improving those skills. A final advantage is that many of these games require multiple players, which doubles the opportunity to learn, promotes discussion, and lets you benefit from the knowledge of others.

There are other kinds of fun and productive study aids. Some, such as flash cards, are helpful for testing basic facts. Others are great for gathering interesting geo-tidbits. These should be treated as supplements to your learning.

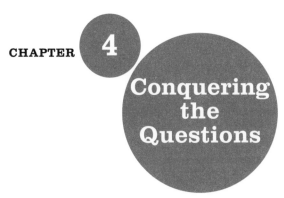

CHAPTER 4

Conquering the Questions

Genius is one percent inspiration and ninety-nine percent perspiration.
—THOMAS ALVA EDISON

This chapter presents questions that have been used at the school, state, and national levels of the Bee. Most are from the preliminary competitions, as questions there are organized by geographic categories. Samples of map, graph, and photo questions are also included.

The objective here is not to provide questions and answers for you to memorize. Rather, it is to make you familiar with the kinds of questions asked in the Bee and show you how to look for clues within the questions that can help you come up with the right answers. Learning how to recognize the clues will reinforce the need to master the ten study tips outlined in Chapter 3. It is important to remember that the purpose of the Bee is to test your knowledge of geography. This means you don't have to worry about "trick" questions. Just take your time and think things through. Even if you answer incorrectly, you will learn something new for next time.

Before plunging into the questions, here are a few pointers to remember about the contest. First, remember the Bee is usually an oral competition (except for the written Qualifying Test that each school champion takes), so you won't have the benefit of seeing the questions in writing. It is important to listen carefully. The moderator will read each question only once, and you want to be sure to hear all the clues that might help you answer correctly.

Second, be sure to listen to the entire question before answering. Don't assume that you know what is going to be asked. You have only one chance to respond. Once you say an answer out loud, it is very unlikely that you will have time to change it before the moderator responds.

Third, don't let difficult-sounding words intimidate or sidetrack you. If the moderator trips over the pronunciation, he or she should automatically repeat the entire question. If you think having a word spelled will help you, then ask the moderator to spell it out. Just be aware that you can interrupt the competition only two times to ask either to have a question repeated or a word spelled. This rule applies to the Preliminary Competition and to the Final Round at each level of the Bee.

Finally, always speak very clearly with your best pronunciation. Don't worry if microphones are present, because they make you sound very cool and extra important!

Some Bee rounds involve questions from a single topic, such as cultural geography; others are a mix of many topics. The first few rounds usually offer a choice of two answers so that you have a 50-50 chance of answering correctly. This is to help you relax.

Gradually, the questions become more difficult as you progress from round to round and from one level to the next. After all, the Bee is a contest, and ultimately only one student can be the champion. But if you stay cool, use your study tips, and look for clues, you'll be surprised at how many questions you will be able to answer correctly.

The questions that follow are organized first by the level of the Bee in which they were used, and then by the round in which they appeared. Since the titles of rounds can change from year to year, and since the sample questions are taken from several different years, the titles listed here are only representative of what you might encounter. You may also notice that some questions could fit in more than one category. This overlap is just the nature of geography. The round titles will give you a general idea of the focus of the questions included in them. The first question in each round is followed by a discussion in italics that points out clues and reminds you of the study tips that will lead you to the correct answer (in bold type). For the remaining questions in the round you are on your own. You will find the answers starting on page 123.

As you go through the questions, jot down new terms, facts, and place-names. Keep your study tools handy so you can put questions in their geographic context. Try timing yourself to get practice in answering within the 15-second time limit (12 seconds for the national Final Round questions). Since the Bee is usually an oral competition, consider having someone read the questions to you. That will teach you to listen carefully for clues. Most of all, have fun!

Round 1: U.S. Geography

1. Which state has areas that are prone to avalanches—Colorado or Kansas?

The word "avalanches" is the clue here. From studying geographic terms, you know they are moving masses of snow that occur in high mountains. From your physical maps you know that Colorado has lots of mountains, so you correctly answer **Colorado.**

2. Which state has a predominantly arid climate—Tennessee or New Mexico?

3. The Great Plains and the Rocky Mountains are two major physical features in which state—Montana or Minnesota?

4. The geographic center of the lower 48 states lies in which state—Kansas or Idaho?

5. Hoover Dam, located on the Arizona-Nevada border, forms a large reservoir on which river—the Platte River or the Colorado River?

6. Which national park is located in a desert region—Yosemite National Park or Saguaro [suh-WAH-roh] National Park?

7. Which state borders two of the Great Lakes—New York or Delaware?

8. Which state has a humid subtropical climate—South Carolina or South Dakota?

9. Hells Canyon, the deepest gorge in the United States, borders Idaho and which state—Oregon or Nebraska?

10. Which state is made up of eight main islands—Hawai'i or Rhode Island?

11. Which is the largest U.S. lake west of the Mississippi River— Lake Mead or the Great Salt Lake?

12. Which city is located on the northeastern shore of San Francisco Bay – Oakland or Phoenix?

Round 2: Geographic Comparisons in the United States

1. Which state has a larger Hispanic population in terms of numbers—California or Wisconsin?

You know that many Hispanic people speak Spanish as their primary language. From keeping up with current events you know that most Hispanic people in the United States come into the country from Mexico, a country that borders California. From studying place-names you also know that many cities in California have Spanish names. So you correctly answer **California.**

2. Which city is located closer to sea level—Denver or Los Angeles?

3. Which state is more likely to experience a blizzard—Idaho or Arkansas?

4. Which state is located closer to the Bay of Fundy—North Carolina or Maine?

5. Which state has more land used for agriculture—Illinois or New Jersey?

6. Which state has a lower average elevation—Arkansas or Florida?

7. Which state grows more rice—Pennsylvania or Louisiana?

8. Which state capital is located closer to the Atlantic Ocean— Springfield or Richmond?

9. Which state has more miles of interstate highways—California or South Dakota?

10. Which state has a *longer* border with Mexico—Texas or California?

11. Which state is *farther* from the Mississippi River—Indiana or West Virginia?

12. Which state is more likely to experience a tornado—New York or Oklahoma?

Round 3: Odd One Out

1. Which country does *not* border the Atlantic Ocean—Mauritania, Cameroon, or Tanzania?

Drawing on your mental map of Africa, you know that the Atlantic Ocean borders the west coast where Mauritania and Cameroon are located, while the Indian Ocean borders the east coast where Tanzania is. So, you correctly answer **Tanzania.**

2. Which country does *not* have land in the subarctic climate zone—France, Finland, or Sweden?

3. Which country is *not* crossed by the Nile River—Namibia, Egypt, or Sudan?

4. Which country is *not* landlocked—Papua New Guinea, Mali, or Belarus?

5. Which country is *not* made up of a group of islands—Japan, Thailand, or the Philippines?

6. Which country in *not* in Europe—Poland, Uzbekistan, or Romania?

7. Which country is *not* located in the Caribbean—Bahamas, Seychelles, or Barbados?

8. Which country does *not* have a canal linking two major bodies of water—Mexico, Panama, or Egypt?

9. Which country does *not* border Russia—Mongolia, Romania, or Ukraine?

10. Which country does *not* include part of the Sahara—Algeria, Botswana, or Libya?

11. Which country is *not* a major producer of petroleum—Algeria, France, or Saudi Arabia?

12. Which country does *not* border the Arctic Ocean—Canada, Russia, or Sweden?

Round 4: Cultural Geography

1. Spices such as cinnamon, cumin, chili, and turmeric have been used not only as flavoring but also as medicine in South Asia's largest country. Name this country.

From studying political regions in your atlases, you know that South Asia is usually considered to include India, Pakistan, Bangladesh, Nepal, and Bhutan. A quick check of your mental map tells you which is the largest, so you correctly answer **India.**

2. The samba, which was originally brought from Africa, is a dance that was adapted and is highly popular on which other continent?

3. In ancient times the papyrus plant, used for making paper, grew along the Nile River Delta in which country?

4. Highway signs in both Gaelic and English are common in which country?

5. The Yorkshire terrier was named for a region in which country in Western Europe?

6. The Malagasy have strong ties with the French and live on the largest island in the Indian Ocean. Name this island.

7. Which country moved its capital from Istanbul to the more centrally located Ankara in the early 20th century?

8. Part of the Spanish colonial empire until 1898, which Southeast Asian island country is predominantly Roman Catholic?

9. To visit the home of the famous painter Rubens and to walk through the world's largest diamond district in Antwerp, you would travel to what country?

10. Hakas, dances meant to frighten enemies, are a traditional part of the Maori culture in which island nation?

11. Afrikaners are the descendants of European settlers who mostly live in which present-day African country?

12. Potatoes were first cultivated more than a thousand years ago by people living in which mountain system in the Western Hemisphere?

Round 5: Continents

1. Scientists believe that about 120 million years ago, South America began to break away from which other continent?
*From learning about plate tectonics and from studying the shapes of continents and their positions in relationship to each other, you correctly answer **Africa**.*

2. The North Atlantic current brings warm waters from the tropics to the west coast of which continent?

3. Both the prime meridian and the Equator cross which continent?

4. The Bellingshausen [BEH-lings-HOW-zen] Sea and the Ross Sea both border which continent?

5. The Great Dividing Range lies in the eastern part of which continent?

6. Which continent produces the largest total amount of rice?

7. Chinchillas and llamas are native to which continent?

8. Which continent is second largest in area?

9. The Benelux Countries get their name from the first letters of three small countries located on what continent?

10. The Middle East serves as a crossroads between Asia, Africa, and what other continent?

11. The world's longest coral reef is in the Pacific Ocean off the northeast coast of which continent?

12. The Gulf Stream is an ocean current that flows along the eastern coast of which continent?

Round 6: Physical Geography

1. What is the term for a part of an ocean or sea that cuts far into the bordering landmass and may contain one or more bays?
From studying physical features on maps and using your geographical reference book, you narrow your choices to two terms: bay and gulf. Since the word "bay" is used in the question, you eliminate it as a possibility and correctly answer **gulf.**

2. The study of the processes in Earth's atmosphere that produce day-to-day weather is called what?

3. What is the term for a narrow, natural waterway that connects two larger bodies of water?

4. An archipelago [ar-kuh-PEH-luh-goh] is a group of what physical features found in a body of water?

5. What term is used for the type of heat energy within the Earth that can be used to generate electricity?

6. What theory explains the shifting positions and ongoing movements of the continents?

7. What Norwegian word is used for a narrow, steep-sided inlet of the sea that was carved by a glacier?

8. What term is used for the often triangular-shaped deposit of sediment sometimes found at the mouth of a river?

9. What is the term for the point on Earth's surface directly above the place where an earthquake originates?

10. A moraine is made up of soil, rocks, and other materials that have been deposited by the action of what kind of physical feature?

11. What is the term for the ecosystem generally consisting of broadleaf evergreen trees that is found in wet tropical areas such as the Amazon basin?

12. What is the term for an area of desert where an underground water source supports vegetation growth?

Round 7: World Geography

1. The Vistula River and Bialowieza National Park—northern Europe's largest area of virgin forest and home to the European bison—are in which country?

Here is where you might want to ask the moderator to spell a word. The spelling and the pronunciation are clues to the country where it is located. But a bigger clue is the Vistula River. From studying country profiles and physical maps you know that the Vistula is the chief river in **Poland.**

2. The port of Rotterdam is built on the delta of which major European river?

3. Mumbai is a major port city in which country that has a population of more than one billion people?

4. Over two million barrels of oil a day are exported from what South American country with a border on the Caribbean Sea?

5. The Gaza Strip and the West Bank are territories bordering what country on the Mediterranean coast of Southwest Asia?

6. Serengeti National Park, a vast grassland southeast of Lake Victoria, was established in 1951 in which country?

7. Gold and uranium are found in the Outback, an interior region of which country bordering on the Pacific and Indian Oceans?

8. Hadrian's Wall, a defensive structure built by the Romans, stretches across which country?

9. Invaded by Turkish forces in 1974, which Mediterranean island is divided between the Turkish-controlled north and the Greek south?

10. Which landlocked European country, a grand duchy, is surrounded by Belgium, Germany, and France?

11. Which West African nation, east of Liberia, is the largest cocoa producer in the world?

12. The Central Asian nations of Turkmenistan, Uzbekistan, and Tajikistan all border what landlocked country in the Hindu Kush Mountains?

Tiebreaker Questions

1. The Tropic of Capricorn passes through the largest island in the Indian Ocean. Name this island.

You know from studying lines of latitude that the Tropic of Capricorn is 23¹/₂° south of the Equator. From your mental maps you know that the Indian Ocean lies between Africa and Australia. Running down your list of the world's 10 largest islands, you correctly answer **Madagascar.**

2. Tibetan legend says that a mysterious creature called a yeti roams the snowy slopes of what mountain range?

3. Which U.S. state has the most votes in the electoral college, because it has the largest population and the most members of Congress?

4. According to tradition, a small country located in a mountainous region of Italy was settled by Christians escaping persecution in the fourth century. Name this country.

5. The Bass Strait separates mainland Australia from which island?

6. What feature on a map allows people to calculate the actual distance between two places shown on the map?

7. What language is spoken by more Chinese than any other language?

8. Ceylon tea is grown on hillsides of what South Asian country?

SCHOOL-LEVEL FINAL ROUND

The questions in the Final Round are similar to those in the Preliminary Competition, except they are more difficult. The questions are not grouped into geographic categories. Instead, it is a good bet that each question will test your knowledge about a different geographic subject. The exception to this is the series of questions that pertains to a map, graph, or other visual aid.

Map Questions

To answer the questions below, you will have to use the map showing major U.S. rivers on the facing page. This round tests your ability to identify U.S. states from their shapes. Knowing where the rivers are located will save you valuable time in reading the map and figuring out the answer to each question.

1. The Susquehanna [sus kwah-HA-nah] begins in which state?

2. The Ohio River forms the entire border between Indiana and which state?

3. The Sacramento River empties into the Pacific Ocean in which state?

4. The Chattahoochee [chat-uh-HOO-chee] River begins in which state?

5. The Arkansas River begins in which state?

6. The Platte River joins the Missouri River just south of Omaha in which state?

7. The Connecticut River forms much of the border between Vermont and which state?

8. The Savannah River forms the border between Georgia and which state?

Major Rivers of the United States

Yukon

Sacramento
San Joaquin
Columbia
Colorado
Snake
Missouri
Rio Grande
Platte
Brazos
Red
Arkansas
Mississippi
Tennessee
Ohio
Chattahoochee
Savannah
Susquehanna
Hudson
Connecticut

NATIONAL
GEOGRAPHIC

QUALIFYING TEST

The Qualifying Test is the only part of the Bee that is completely written. Its 70 questions, including a set pertaining to a map, graph, or other visual aid, cover a wide variety of geographic topics. Each question offers a choice of four answers, and you must choose the number (1, 2, 3, or 4) that you believe identifies the correct answer. Remember, the only time that you will take this test is if you are the winner of your School Bee.

1. The Olmec, one of Middle America's first civilizations, lived in a region bordering which body of water?

Gulf of California   1
Gulf of Mexico   2
Caribbean Sea   3
Chesapeake Bay   4

The Middle America clue eliminates Chesapeake Bay. You know that some of the earliest civilizations were in southern Mexico, so you correctly answer **2.**

2. What is the name of the Dutch explorer who, in 1642, became the first European to sight New Zealand?

Prince Henry the Navigator 1
James Cook   2
Ferdinand Magellan   3
Abel Tasman   4

3. Which city is part of a major industrial region in Japan?

Hong Kong	1
Osaka	2
Seoul	3
Taipei	4

4. Which people have historically used outrigger and double canoes to travel great distances over open seas?

Bedouin	1
San	2
Polynesians	3
Vikings	4

5. Which Caribbean island has oil-refining centers at San Fernando and Pointe-à-Pierre?

Cuba	1
Jamaica	2
Trinidad	3
Hispaniola	4

6. The dinar is the official currency of several countries in which region?

Caribbean Sea	1
Middle East	2
Pacific Rim	3
Sub-Saharan Africa	4

7. The forum was the central gathering place in the cities of which culture?

Roman	1
Danish	2
Russian	3
French	4

8. In 1838, the Cherokee Indians followed the Trail of Tears in a forced migration from Tennessee to which state?

Arizona	1
Texas	2
Colorado	3
Oklahoma	4

9. About 90 percent of Poland's people adhere to which religion?

Buddhism	1
Hinduism	2
Islam	3
Christianity	4

Analogies

The Qualifying Test almost always has a series of analogies in which you are asked to compare two things that have something in common. For example, in the analogy "The peso is to Mexico as the WHAT is to Japan?" the answer is yen because yen is the currency of Japan, just as the peso is the currency in Mexico. See if you can figure out the following analogies.

10. Mining is to primary economic activity as WHAT is to secondary economic activity?

banking	1
fishing	2
manufacturing	3
education	4

11. Cyrillic is to Russian as kanji and kana characters are to WHAT?

Arabic	1
Japanese	2
Latin	3
Gaelic	4

12. Saigon is to Ho Chi Minh City as Bombay is to WHAT?

Melbourne	1
Istanbul	2
Bucharest	3
Mumbai	4

13. A compass is to direction as an anemometer is to WHAT?

ocean depth	1
elevation	2
atmospheric pressure	3
wind speed	4

Graph Questions

Use the climate graphs (opposite page) to answer these questions.

14. Which climate graph represents a hot desert region?

    A   1
    B   2
    C   3
    D   4

You know that a desert by definition has very little rain, and the question tells you that it is a hot desert. Looking at the graphs, you see that there are two that have little rainfall (C and D), but only one of these (C) has high temperatures, so you correctly answer **3.**

15. Which climate graph best illustrates a high-latitude location in the Northern Hemisphere?

    A   1
    B   2
    C   3
    D   4

16. Which type of vegetation would you most likely find in climate graph B?

    tropical rain forest   1
    desert   2
    tundra   3
    coniferous forest   4

These climate graphs represent climate regions in various parts of the world. Each uses a bar graph (black) to indicate the average amount of monthly precipitation, and a line graph (gray) to indicate the average monthly temperature. The gray numbers represent temperatures in degrees Fahrenheit. The black numbers represent amount of precipitation in inches. The letters along the bottom of each graph stand for the months of the year beginning with January.

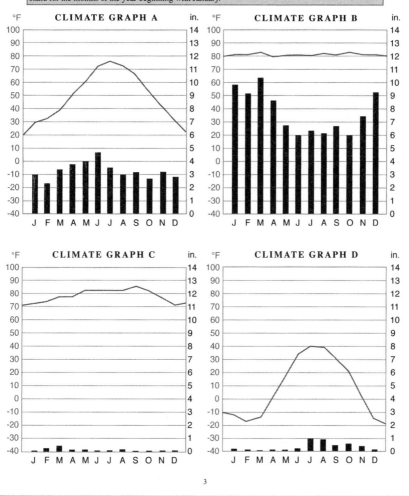

3

STATE-LEVEL PRELIMINARY ROUNDS

At the state level, before the official questioning begins, there is a warm-up round to help you relax. Your answers to these questions do not count. As with the school level, the first few rounds at the state offer a choice of answers.

Round 1: Cultural Geography

1. Which country has the world's largest Muslim population—Indonesia or Mexico?

If you have studied maps showing world religions you will know the answer immediately. If you haven't, you might reason that Mexico was settled by the Spanish, followers of Christianity not Islam. Either way, you correctly answer **Indonesia.**

2. Which country has more people who speak a Germanic language—Denmark or Azerbaijan?

3. La Boca [lah BOH-kah] is an Italian neighborhood in Argentina's most populous city. Name this port city.

4. Which Central American country located just northwest of El Salvador has 23 officially recognized indigenous languages?

5. The hangul, a 24-letter alphabet, is used to write the language of two countries on a peninsula that borders the Yellow Sea. Name this *peninsula*.

6. Conflict between the Bhote [VOTE-ay] and the Nepalese ethnic groups has caused large refugee movements away from the smallest country in the Himalaya. Name this country.

7. People in the most populous Scandinavian country celebrate a festival of lights called St. Lucia [loo-SEE-uh] Day to mark the start of the Christmas season. Name this country.

8. Sanskrit, preserved in Hindu sacred writings, is an ancient language in which country?

9. The Gold Museum, which contains a large collection of pre-Columbian gold objects, is the capital city east of the Magdalena [MAG-dah-LAY-nah] River. Name this city.

10. Some of the oldest sagas, which are based on history and legends, were written in the 13th century in what island country in the North Atlantic?

Round 2: Physical Geography

1. Which term describes a body of water that occasionally or seasonally dries up—intermittent or brackish?
*The words "occasionally" and "seasonally" suggest not continuous, so you correctly answer **intermittent**.*

2. In high mountain areas, rocks are often weathered by which process—frost action or wave refraction?

3. Which term is used for a circular coral reef island that surrounds a lagoon—atoll or abyss?

4. Which type of climate is characterized by dry summers and mild, wet winters—tropical wet or Mediterranean?

5. Which term describes the point at which two streams meet—fissure or confluence?

6. What is the term for the solid rock that lies underneath sand, clay, or other loose material—caprock or bedrock?

7. What term describes a narrow, fast-moving wind current found at high altitudes – doldrums or jet stream?

8. What is the term for a geoscientist who studies earthquakes—seismologist or meteorologist?

9. What term describes the seasonal shift in wind direction that brings alternate very wet and very dry seasons to India and much of Southeast Asia—monsoon or El Niño?

10. What is the term for a layer of permeable rock that contains water—aquifer or caldera?

Round 3: Odd Item Out

1. Which country is *not* part of the Southern Cone region in South America— Argentina, Chile, or Ecuador?

*Using your mental map of South America, you know that Chile and Argentina are neighboring countries that extend to the southern tip of South America. Ecuador, on the other hand, straddles the Equator in the northern part of the continent. You conclude that the correct answer is **Ecuador**.*

2. Which country does *not* extend west of the Prime Meridian— Austria, Ireland, or Spain?

3. Which country does *not* use Spanish as an official language— Paraguay, Suriname [soor-uh-NAHM], or Guatemala?

4. Which country does *not* include part of the Sahel region— Sudan, Mali, or Morocco?

5. Which of the following mountain ranges is *not* in Europe—the Pyrenees, Apennines, or Pamirs [puh-MEERZ]?

6. Which of the following islands is *not* part of Indonesia—Luzon [loo-ZON], Sumatra, or Java?

7. Which of the following is *not* a trench found in the Pacific Ocean—the Aleutian Trench, the Puerto Rico Trench, or the Philippine Trench?

8. Which African country does *not* border Lake Victoria—Ethiopia, Kenya, or Uganda?

9. Which country is *not* crossed by the Equator—Chad, Colombia, or Indonesia?

10. Which country was *not* a British colony—Cambodia, Myanmar, or Malaysia?

11. Which country does *not* have any savanna—Tanzania, Kenya, or Libya?

12. Which country does *not* border the Black Sea—Georgia, Turkey, or Turkmenistan?

Round 4: Economic Geography

1. Which Canadian province produces more than half of the country's manufactured goods?
You know from your mental maps that Ontario borders all of the Great Lakes and has access to the St. Lawrence Seaway. This puts it in a better position than any other Canadian province to import materials needed for manufacturing and to export finished goods. So you correctly answer **Ontario.**

2. The leading grain crop in Bangladesh is a staple food for the country's people. Name this grain.

3. Spain's chief industrial city is a Mediterranean port near the country's border with France. Name this city.

4. Most of Denmark's oil reserves are found in which sea?

5. Sunflower oil produced from crops that grow north of Sofia, a city located in which European country?

6. The rail tunnel beneath the English Channel connects the island of Great Britain to which country?

7. The country that borders both the Gulf of Oman and the Caspian Sea is the world's leading producer of pistachio nuts. Name this country.

8. Oil located near the coast of the states of Tabasco and Veracruz is a valuable resource for which Latin American country?

9. A British overseas territory in the Caribbean Sea with George Town as its capital is known as a major offshore center for finance. Name this island group.

10. Which East African country that straddles the Equator and borders the Indian Ocean is known for its exports of coffee, tea, and flowers?

Round 5: Current Events

The questions in this round assume that you are keeping up with events in the news. If you are, then chances are, coming up with the answers will be easy. Just in case you aren't, you'll find location clues that will help you come up with the correct answer.

1. In October 2006, the European Commission urged an island country east of Greenland to reconsider its decision to resume commercial whale hunting. Name this country.

2. In September 2006, a military-led coup removed Prime Minister Thaksin Shinawatra [TAKK-sihn shih-nah-WAHT-ruh] from power in the only Asian country not colonized by a European power. Name this country.

3. In October 2006, scientists announced the discovery of 150 million-year-old fossils belonging to giant sea reptiles in the Svalbard archipelago. The Svalbard archipelago is part of which European country?

4. In December 2006, a military commander seized control of what country composed of over 300 islands in the Pacific Ocean whose capital is Suva?

5. In November 2006, Pierre Gemayel, a Lebanese cabinet minister, was assassinated after opposing political influence in Lebanon by what neighboring country, whose capital is Damascus?

6. In October 2006, Muhammad Yunus and the Grameen Bank were jointly awarded the 2006 Nobel Peace Prize for micro-credit lending schemes in what country bordered by India and the Bay of Bengal?

7. In December 2006, world leaders met in the United States to mobilize efforts to fight malaria. Thousands of children are affected by malaria annually in what African country bordering Somalia that is crossed by the Equator?

8. In November 2006, Pope Benedict XVI celebrated Mass near ruins of Ephesus at one of Christianity's holiest sites. What mostly Muslim country, whose largest city is Istanbul, did the Pope visit?

9. In October 2006, President Evo Morales announced that he would nationalize the mines in his country, which is located east of Lake Titicaca. Name this country.

10. In November 2006, the toy company Lego announced plans to move manufacturing plants to Mexico and the Czech Republic from Billund, a town in what southernmost Scandinavian country?

11. In December 2006, Sultan Mizan Zainal Abidan was crowned 13th ruler of a country located across the Johore Strait from Singapore. Name this country.

Round 6: Historical Geography

1. To visit the ruins of Persepolis, an ancient ceremonial capital of Persia, you would have to travel to what present-day country?
From history books or from studying country profiles, you know that Persia is the former name of Iran, so you correctly answer **Iran.**

2. The Central Powers, an alliance that included Germany, Austria-Hungary, Bulgaria, and the Ottoman Empire, fought together during which major European conflict?

3. What Asian trading port, formerly controlled by the Dutch East India Company, was known as Batavia until 1949?

4. Prior to the construction of the Panama Canal, Chile's present-day largest port served as a stop-off point for ships traveling around Cape Horn in the Pacific Ocean. Name this city.

5. Name the vast, mineral-rich region that stretches from the Ural Mountains to the Bering Sea that was conquered in part by the Cossacks during the reign of Ivan the Terrible.

6. The Battle of Sobraon [soh-BROWN] in 1846 was fought between the British forces and the Sikhs in which present-day country?

7. Since gaining independence from Spain in 1825, a South American country with two capitals has experienced nearly 200 revolutions or military coups. Name this country.

8. Thonburi, located on the Chao Phraya [chow PRYE-uh] River, was the temporary capital of what present-day country from 1767-1782?

9. The Soviet Union's 1948 blockade of the western section of a German city led to a 15-month airlift by Western Allies. Name this city.

10. Carthage, once a Phoenician settlement and later a Roman city, is located in which African country?

11. In 1801, an Act of Union created the United Kingdom by joining Great Britain and which other island?

12. The ancient kingdom of Kush adopted elements of Egyptian art, language, and religion. Kush was located in which present-day country?

Round 7: Political Geography

1. The large Danish island of Kalaallit Nunaat, which borders the Arctic and Atlantic Oceans, is more commonly known by what other name?

A check of your mental map of the world and of the list of 10 largest islands reveals that there is only one large island that borders both the Arctic and Atlantic Oceans. Even if you don't know that it belongs to Denmark, you know the answer must be **Greenland.**

2. Name *one* of the two South American countries that have territorial claims in Antarctica.

3. What present-day landlocked country in Southeast Asia was under the control of Siam, present-day Thailand, at the beginning of the 19th century?

4. Angola and Mozambique, both located in sub-Saharan Africa, gained independence in 1975 from which Iberian country?

5. KwaZulu-Natal province, located on the Indian Ocean, is the most populous province in which country bordering Botswana?

6. Ceuta [see-YOO-tuh], once known for its trade in ivory, gold, and slaves, is located on Morocco's Mediterranean coast and is an exclave of which country?

7. The Yalu River, which originates in the Changbai [CHANG-BEI] Mountains and empties into the Yellow Sea, forms part of the boundary between China and which other country?

8. New Brunswick, bordering the Bay of Fundy, is a province of what country?

9. The Windward Passage, which connects the Atlantic Ocean and the Caribbean Sea, separates Haiti from which neighboring country?

10. Which country, bordering Congo, is crossed by the Equator and became independent of France in 1960?

Tiebreaker Questions

1. Name the country that controls the straits that connect the Mediterranean and Black Seas.

From your mental physical maps you know that these straits are at the eastern end of the Mediterranean Sea. Your mental political map of the region shows you that only one country borders both the Black Sea and the Mediterranean Sea. Reasoning that this country would control the straits, you correctly answer **Turkey.**

2. In 1667, the Dutch ceded New Amsterdam to the British in return for what present-day South American country?

3. The Pillars of Hercules, named after a hero of ancient Greek mythology, mark the eastern entrance of what strategically important strait?

4. The most populous city in Azerbaijan is located on a peninsula that stretches into the Caspian Sea. Name this port city.

5. Name the area of the North Atlantic Ocean that takes its name from a kind of seaweed that flourishes there.

6. The capital of Belarus is also the administrative headquarters of the Commonwealth of Independent States. Name this city.

7. The Islamic university in Fez is one of the oldest universities in the world. This institution is located in which North African country?

8. Known for its Blue Mountains, which country is the third largest island in the Caribbean?

STATE-LEVEL FINAL ROUND

The only rounds of questions organized by topics in the State Finals are those that deal with a theme or visual materials, such as maps, graphs, or photographs. The following randomly selected examples are designed to give you an idea of what you can expect for these kinds of rounds.

Oral Analogies

This series of questions requires you to complete an analogy by providing the missing element. Here is an example of an analogy: Mount McKinley is to North America as Mount Everest is to WHAT? Mount McKinley is the highest peak on the continent of North America, and Mount Everest is the highest peak in Asia, so the answer is Asia.

1. St. John's is to Antigua and Barbuda as Port-of-Spain is to WHAT?

2. The Indus River is to Pakistan as the Orinoco River is to WHAT?

3. Tikal is to Guatemala as Machu Picchu is to WHAT?

4. The Malagasy Republic is to Madagascar as Siam is to WHAT?

5. Lake Managua is to Nicaragua as Great Slave Lake is to WHAT?

6. Siberia is to Russia as Moravia is to WHAT?

7. Mont Bagzane [BAHG-zahn] is to Niger as Kilimanjaro is to WHAT?

8. East Pakistan is to Bangladesh as Upper Volta is to WHAT?

9. The Bekaa Valley is to Lebanon as the Kathmandu Valley is to WHAT?

10. The Cook Islands are to New Zealand as the Faroe Islands are to WHAT?

11. Colón is to Panama as Port Said [sah-EED] is to WHAT?

12. The Taklimakan is to China as the Nubian Desert is to WHAT?

Photo Questions

1. What term describes this type of topography in Guilin [gwee-lin], China, which is characterized by limestone formations, caves, and underground streams?

2. Chicken vendors, shown here, populate the land where former Soviet leader Joseph Stalin was born. Name this present-day Asian country on the east coast of the Black Sea.

3. The people shown here belong to the Yedina tribe, who inhabit the islands and marshy shores of a shrinking African lake. This lake is located near the junction of Cameroon, Nigeria, Niger, and what other country?

4. Over the past 100 years, more than 80 percent of the ice has melted from the summit of Mount Kilimanjaro in which country?

Map Questions

To answer the questions in this series, you will need to refer to the earthquake map on the opposite page. Each question requires two answers: the name of the city and the number that represents it on the map. You must answer both parts of the question correctly to receive credit.

1. A 1948 earthquake killed a large percentage of the population in Turkmenistan's largest city. Give the number and name of this city.

2. Following a 1995 earthquake, broken gas lines started fires that destroyed large sections of Japan's largest container port, located on the western side of Osaka Bay. Give the number and name of this city.

3. In 1972, the largest city in Nicaragua was evacuated after a series of powerful earthquakes struck the downtown area and leveled approximately 80 percent of the buildings. Give the number and name of this city.

4. In 1755, an earthquake almost completely destroyed a settlement in northern Africa that has since become Morocco's largest city. Give the number and name of this city.

5. In 2001, a major earthquake struck southern Peru and damaged historic buildings in one of its largest cities, located at the foot of Volcán Misti. Give the number and name of this city.

Earthquakes

NATIONAL
GEOGRAPHIC

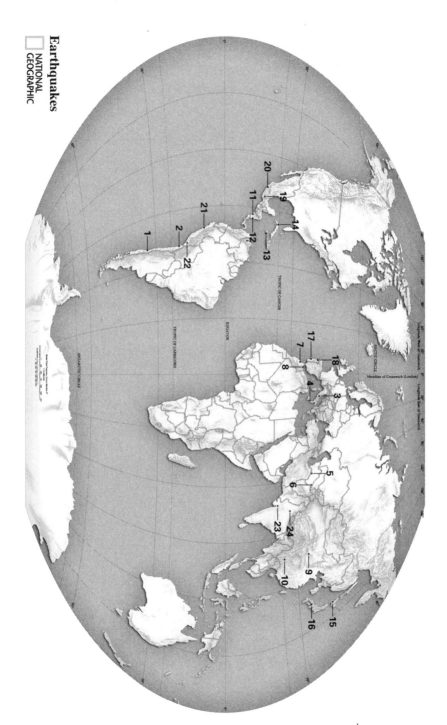

CONQUERING THE QUESTIONS | PAGE 95

NATIONAL-LEVEL PRELIMINARY ROUNDS

The following questions are representative of the questions and geographic categories in the National Preliminary Competition.

Round 1: World Geography

1. The Gulf of Riga [REE-gah] is part of which European Sea?

2. Name the mountain range that stretches from the Bay of Biscay to the Mediterranean Sea.

3. What country that borders Guatemala has English as its official language?

Round 2: Economic Geography

1. Douala [doo-AH-lah], located near the Gulf of Guinea, is the most important seaport of which African country?

2. Phosphates are exported from Aqaba [AH-kuh-buh], the only major port in which Asian country?

3. Santos, the world's leading coffee-exporting port, is in which country?

Round 3: Cultural Geography

1. The Ha'Penny [HAY-pen-ee] Bridge is a nearly 200-year-old pedestrian bridge across the River Liffey in which western European capital city?

2. Thessaloníki, or Salonica, is a city named for the wife of an ancient Macedonian king. This city is in what country?

3. Wood-carvers are commissioned to make elaborate coffins in the shape of animals, cars, and other objects in which African country just west of Togo?

Round 4: General Geography

1. Place these cities in order according to their average annual rainfall from *most* to *least:* Kabul, Belize City, Sydney.

2. Place these countries in order according to the length of their coastlines, from *longest* to *shortest:* Pakistan, Cambodia, China.

3. Place these countries in order of their land area from *largest* to *smallest:* Angola, Kenya, Nigeria.

Round 5: Physical Geography

1. In the southwestern United States, a Spanish word is commonly used for a streambed that is usually dry except after heavy rains. What is this term?

2. What is the term for the broad crater formed when an eruption destroys the upper part of a volcanic cone or when the cone collapses inward?

3. What is the term for a body of water enclosed by an atoll?

CHAPTER **5**

Tips From Bee Finalists

I now think almost anything is possible if I work hard enough.
—NICHOLAS JACHOWSKI
HAWAII STATE BEE
CHAMPION, 2001

This chapter provides advice from school and state champions about when to get involved, what to study, and how to relax. Although some of the contributors are now in high school, at one time or another they were all Bee kids just like you. So listen up!

●●●●●●●●●●●●●●●●●●●●●●●●●●●

Don't be overwhelmed by all the things you need to know. Tackle geography step by step. Just about anything can pop up in a Bee question, but I would recommend starting with the most important and essential information first: the continents, countries, and capitals, then move on to their major physical features, which include mountains, deserts, lowlands, oceans, gulfs, bays, straits, rivers, lakes, islands, and other types of landforms. From there you add in layers of complexity, including the study of major cities, regions, languages, ethnicities, religions, and currencies. Next, become familiar with where natural resources and certain agricultural products are produced. Then add the historical high-lights and political system of each country. Try to study at least a few hours a day to retain all the knowledge you have gained. Before you know it, you will start building a vast geographic ency-clopedia inside your head!

Caitlin Snaring, 2006, 2007 State Bee Champion, Washington State (7th–8th Grade); 2007 National Champion (8th Grade)

● ●

I believe that what helped me prepare for the Bee the most was my love for reading. By reading lots of books, magazines, and especially newspapers, you can gain a vast knowledge of other places and cul-tures. During the actual Bee, I think the best things to do are listen carefully to the whole question, use the given time to really think about your answer, and be confident when you give your answer.

Rachel Schuerger, 2001 State Bee Champion, Alaska (8th Grade)

● ●

My major tips for the Bee are to STAY CALM during the ques-tions that you are asked, and close your eyes so that you can hear the questions better. Never panic. Just think calmly and coolly about each question. Even if you don't know the answer, most questions can be narrowed down to two choices. Then make an educated guess based on the clues in the question. Never cram the day before the Bee, and make sure to get a good night's sleep.

Krishnan Chandra, 2004–06 State Bee Champion, Massachusetts (6th–8th Grade)

•••••••••••••••••••••••••

Write everything down in notebooks then use them to quiz yourself a little bit each night. Make flashcards of countries and their capitals, territories and their capitals, countries and their currencies, and states and their nicknames. Fill out outline maps of the world, each continent, and each country. Read the newspaper everyday to brush up on your current events, and play geography trivia games on the Internet.

Make sure you make geography fun. But don't make the Bee about winning it all (even though it would be nice) or studying all the time. Get your friends involved in your studying. One of my best friends, who knows very little about geography, always quizzed me on whatever she could think of.

Olivia Colangelo, 2003 School Bee Champion (7th Grade); 2004 State Bee Champion, Pennsylvania (8th Grade)

•••••••••••••••••••••••••

Try to get involved in the school Bees in the fourth grade or as soon as possible. The first couple of years, the competition will be challenging, even discouraging, and not as easy as it looks. You have to put a lot of time and effort into studying geography to really do well. I can't exactly pinpoint just what it is that I like so much about geography, but it is not in any way tedious studying for the Bee.

Erik Bolt, 2001 State Bee Champion, Homeschooler, Indiana (8th Grade)

●●●●●●●●●●●●●●●●●●●●●●●●●

I have always loved learning about people and places, so for me preparing for the Bee was a way to complement the knowledge I had already acquired. I enjoyed every minute I spent reading, poring over maps, memorizing facts, and playing geography-based computer games. My advice is simply to enjoy preparing while learning as much information as possible.

Tom Meyerson, 2003 and 2004 State Bee Champion, District of Columbia (7th and 8th Grades)

●●●●●●●●●●●●●●●●●●●●●●●●●

My best hints to future competitors are to study, study, study, love what you are doing, and make use of the Internet. It's fun, and it's free.

Matthew Vengalil, 2006 State Bee Champion, Michigan (8th Grade)

●●●●●●●●●●●●●●●●●●●●●●●●●

I prepared for the Bee by having my family go through questions in the *National Geographic Bee Official Study Guide, Afghanistan to Zimbabwe,* and *The Geography Bee Complete Preparation Handbook,* looking at atlases, and watching TV programs, especially the History and Travel Channels. Before the competition, I contacted the previous state winner for New Jersey to see what tips he had.

Evan Meltzer, 2006 State Bee Champion, New Jersey (8th Grade)

●●●●●●●●●●●●●●●●●●●●●●●●●●●●

Always make good use of your time, and study regularly. I studied three hours a day on weekdays and eight hours a day on weekends. Try not to just memorize but also to understand. If you can understand the world, this will help you to prepare not only for the Bee but also for a future career and for life.
Neeraj Sirdeshmukh, 2006 State Bee Champion, New Hampshire (8th Grade)

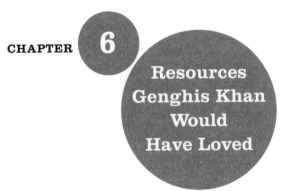

I will leave no stone unturned.
—ARISTOPHANES

CHAPTER **6**

Resources Genghis Khan Would Have Loved

Many centuries ago the great Mongol ruler, Genghis Khan, united his nomad tribes into a formidable army. His Golden Horde swept across the Central Asian steppe on horseback, terrorizing and plundering settlements from the Caspian Sea to the Pacific Ocean. They devastated cities, redirected rivers, and left deserts crowded with fleeing refugees. The Chinese built the Great Wall to keep the "barbarians" out, the Persians hid from them, and the Europeans fell like matchsticks. At the time of Genghis Khan's death in 1227, he controlled one of the greatest land empires the world has ever known.

Mr. Khan succeeded because, unlike the Europeans, his army did not wear heavy armor or burden itself with supply wagons that could break down. The Mongols traveled exceptionally light and fast. Their excellent use of geographic information made this possible. Mongol scouts went out months ahead of the main army, secretly gathering crucial information about terrain, vegetation, and settlements. This later assured the best routes, food for the men and ponies, and great hideaways. In a nutshell (or saddlebag), the Mongol scouts were simply the best.

Although great in the 13th century, Genghis's information was meager compared with what our current atlases, globes, and reference books can provide. Throw in television, the Internet, e-mail, and cell phones that allow instant information to flow around the globe, and you have an advantage that might have turned back even the Golden Horde.

The Mongols aside, just imagine how historic news headlines might have read if our current geographic information and communications technology had been available long ago. We might have seen: "GPS Navigation Guides Columbus to New World (film and details at 11:00)!" "Paul Revere E-Mails Alert from North Church!" "Custer's Lieutenant Faxes Map of Indian Camps." "Cell Phone Saves Captain Scott at South Pole."

The good news today is that for modest barter or a quick crusade to your local library, even ordinary peasants can obtain geographic learning materials the great Khan would have loved (and probably even killed for). An exhaustive list would make a book in itself, so this one simply highlights proven resources that will help you learn to think like a geographer.

ATLASES

Even if you're not scheming to plunder European villages, a good world atlas belongs in every ger, or yurt. This is the standard reference for Bee preparation and should include a full set of political, physical, and thematic maps (population, economic, climate, etc.). Also, look for country profiles, information about the oceans, plate tectonics, time zones, geographic comparisons, etc.

Our rapidly changing world alters the political landscape very quickly, so beware that if your atlas is more than five years old, some country names and boundaries may be outdated. The same is true for population figures and similar statistics. The rule of thumb is always to look for the most recent edition. Also, check to see if a less expensive paperback edition is available.

Large World Atlases

National Geographic Atlas of the World, 8th Edition. National Geographic Society, Washington, DC, 2004.

A superb collection of political, physical, urban, regional, and ocean-floor maps; thematic maps covering topics such as climate patterns, plate tectonics, population, economic trends, and world cultures; country profiles; satellite imagery; temperature and rainfall; geographic comparisons; and a comprehensive index.

Midsize World Atlases

National Geographic Family Reference Atlas of the World, 2nd Edition. National Geographic Society, Washington, DC, 2007.

A comprehensive, family-friendly atlas with sections about the world, continents, oceans, and space. It includes an expansive thematic section with maps, graphs, charts, photographs, and an extensive list of geographic comparisons.

Rand McNally Goode's World Atlas, 21st Edition.
Rand McNally & Co., Skokie, IL, 2006.
A comprehensive world atlas that includes a wide variety of thematic maps; world and regional maps; geographic comparison tables, and explanations of map scale, map projections, and Earth-Sun relationships.

National Geographic Collegiate Atlas of the World. National Geographic Society, Washington, DC, 2006.
This detailed atlas features excellent world and regional maps. The many thematic maps (e.g., Health and Literacy, Defense and Conflict, Protected Lands) are a real strength.

Hammond Concise World Atlas, 5th Edition.
Hammond World Atlas Corp., Union, NJ, 2007.
Satellite imagery; terra-scape maps of land and ocean floor terrain; thematic maps and graphs on population, living standards, agriculture and manufacturing, climate, and the environment. A Quick Reference Guide, and city maps are also included.

Children's and Student World Atlases

National Geographic Student Atlas of the World, Revised and Expanded Edition. National Geographic Society, Washington, DC, 2005. (Grades 6–10)
Packed with informative thematic maps that explore the world's physical and human systems, focusing on geology, climate, vegetation, population, economies, food, energy, and mineral

resources. For each continent there are three sets of maps (physical and political, climate and precipitation, population and predominant economies) plus a photo essay. Web sites are included for finding additional information and updating statistics.

National Geographic World Atlas for Young Explorers, 3rd Edition. National Geographic Society, Washington, DC, 2007. (Grades 3–7)
Winner of the *Parents' Choice* Gold Award, this atlas contains world thematic maps, photo essays, satellite images, physical and political maps of each continent, country profiles, geographic comparisons, a glossary, and a comprehensive index. This latest edition has gone interactive, with its own Web site that provides links to a host of photos, videos, games, world music, animal sounds, maps, and more.

Specialty Atlases

National Geographic Atlas of the Middle East, 2nd Edition. National Geographic Society, Washington, DC (available April 2008).
Explores the complex history of the Middle East through maps devoted to topics that include the rise and falls of empires, civilizations, major conflicts, holy sites, and various other significant events that have shaped the region.

Ocean: An Illustrated Atlas, Sylvia A. Earle and Linda Glover. National Geographic Society, Washington, DC, available Fall 2008.

Features 300 detailed maps, photographs, and state-of-the art satellite images. Includes details about climate, weather, currents, tides, and the ocean's living systems as well as essays by experts on topics from deep-sea drilling to predicting El Niño.

National Geographic United States Atlas for Young Explorers, Updated Edition. National Geographic Society, Washington, DC, 2004. (Grades 3–7; 3rd edition available June 2008.)
Superb U.S., state, and regional maps explain the primary geographical relationships in the United States. Third edition features concise state profiles, photographic essays on each region and state, thematic spreads on topics such as natural disasters, immigration, and climate change, and an interactive Web site that provides links to a host of National Geographic photos, videos, games, animal sounds, maps, and more.

National Geographic Atlas of China. National Geographic Society, Washington, DC, 2007.
Featuring more than 300 full-color maps and illustrations, this atlas provides provincial and city coverage, thematic maps on a wide range of topics, including trade, industry, military strength, tourism, religion, and languages, plus a historical time line and travel information.

World Bank Atlas 2006 (World Development Atlas). World Bank, Washington, DC, 2006.
Easy-to-read world maps, tables, and graphs highlight key social,

economic, and environmental data for the world's economies. Topics include infant mortality, gross domestic product, female labor, drinking water, forest cover, and CO_2 emissions.

Student Atlas of World Politics, 6th Edition, John L. Allen. McGraw/Dushkin, Columbus, OH, 2003.
Emphasizes current affairs that reflect recent developments in political geography and international relations. This collection of maps and data is particularly useful for exploring the relationships between geography and world politics.

GEOGRAPHIC REFERENCE BOOKS

Geography of Religion: Where God Lives, Where Pilgrims Walk, by John Esposito, Susan Tyler Hitchcock, Desmond Tutu, and Mpho Tutu. National Geographic Society, Washington, DC, 2004.
This comprehensive reference traces each of the great religions of humankind from its ancient roots to its role in modern life.

National Geographic Almanac of Geography. National Geographic Society, Washington, DC, 2005.
A comprehensive, illustrated reference packed with easy to understand information about our physical world, human culture, and world economy. Hundreds of maps, charts, drawings, and photographs support the text.

Merriam-Webster's Geographical Dictionary, Revised Third Edition. Merriam-Webster, Inc., Springfield, MA, 2007.

Provides an alphabetical listing of more than 54,000 places and features, with concise information about each plus hundreds of maps and tables.

Geographica's World Reference. Laurel Glen Publishing, San Diego, CA, 2000.

Concise information divided into three comprehensive parts: Planet Earth, People and Society, and A–Z Country Listings. Many illustrations and an excellent gazetteer.

Afghanistan to Zimbabwe: Country Facts That Helped Me Win the National Geographic Bee, Andrew Wojtanik. National Geographic Society, Washington, DC, 2005.

This book is full of the facts about 192 countries that the author compiled to help him study for and win the 2004 National Geographic Bee.

Our Fifty States, by Mark H. Bockenhauer and Stephen F. Cunha. National Geographic Society, Washington, DC, 2004.

Organized by geographic regions, this book is packed with specially designed maps and concise essays that explore the history, climate, natural resources, and physical features of each region, state, the District of Columbia, and the territories.

ALMANACS

The World Almanac for Kids 2008, Alan Joyce. World Almanac Books, New York, NY., 2007.

Abundant information on essential topics, such as animals, computers, inventions, movies and television, religion, and sports. This fact book includes many photographs, illustrations, and maps, along with puzzles, brainteasers, and other activities.

The World Almanac and Book of Facts 2008. World Almanac Books, New York, NY, 2007.
A classic annual with a price that drops during the year. Crammed with global facts from farm imports to volcanic activity and baseball batting averages.

National Geographic Almanac of World History, Patricia Daniels and Stephen G. Hyslop. National Geographic Society, Washington, DC 2006 (paperback).
Through essays, detailed maps, charts, and time lines, this book traces world history from the dawn of humanity to the 21st century.

GEOGRAPHY TEXTBOOKS

Fourth through eighth grade social studies textbooks are a great source for learning about geography. As your skills improve, check out the textbooks for more advanced levels. Don't be afraid of college textbooks. Although they are more difficult to read, if you understand geography fundamentals, they offer a comprehensive and advanced tutorial on most topics. You can find these texts in bookstores, especially college and secondhand bookstores. Or surf the Internet for the best bargains (search under "used college textbooks"). College and university libraries shelve textbooks. Many state and community colleges will allow you to obtain a library card so you can borrow books. If a book was published in the last five years, check for a companion Web site with chapter summaries and a dizzying array of self-tests.

LITERATURE

Reading nonfiction books on just about any topic—exploration, sports, survival, wars, biography, even regional cookbooks!—can help expand your geographic knowledge. Even fiction has to have a setting, and most authors carefully research the background for their plots. This means that just about anything you read can add to your geographic knowledge.

CYBERSPACE RESOURCES

There are great stops on our rapidly emerging information super-highway. Beware that URL addresses change frequently. If you have trouble finding any, consult one of the popular Internet search engines, such as Google (www.google.com) or Lycos (www.lycos.com), and simply request the site name. In any search engine, entering key words such as geography games, geography facts, or geography maps, will produce an array of sites to explore and learn about our world.

Check out the main National Geographic Web site— www.nationalgeographic.com—or one of the following: www.nationalgeographic.com/wildworld/ (online atlas of world wildlife and ecosystems) www.nationalgeographic.com/kids-world-atlas (the companion site to *National Geographic World Atlas for Young Explorers,* 3rd Edition)

www.nationalgeographic.com/geobee/ (offers five new National Geographic Bee questions each day)

UN Atlas of the Oceans: www.oceansatlas.org/

An excellent source of readily accessible and hot-off-the-press information about oceans. Designed for government policy experts and students alike, this site provides information relevant to the sustainable development of the oceans, from basic explanations to intricate data sets.

Quintessential Instructional Archive: www.quia.com/dir/geo

Good flash card quiz site, with plenty of other interactive games. Click "Popular Categories" then navigate the pull-down menu to geography for dozens of worthy activities.

World Resources Institute: www.wri.org/

Click on Climate & Energy, and People & Ecosystems.

About Geography: www.geography.about.com

This site offers free downloads and links to other geography sites, outline maps, and current events.

Population Reference Bureau: www.prb.org

The best source for world population, with interactive population pyramids, a quiz, recent news, country data, and links to other sites.

The CIA World Fact Book:
www.cia.gov/library/publications/the-world-factbook/index.html
Downloadable maps, current information, and background data
on every country.

Science at NASA: www.earth.nasa.gov
Click "For Kids Only." This site explores air, water, land, and hazards at a level useful for Bee contestants.

United Nations: www.un.org
Full of country facts, statistics, current events, maps, and more.

Newspapers online: www.newspapers.com/index.htm
and http://library.uncg.edu/news/
These two sites feature 7,000 links to all of the world's online
newspapers and other sources of information. A great source for
current events from a global perspective. Many are published in
languages native to the region, but nearly every highly populated
country and many regional papers offer an English edition.

Environment Canada: www.cws-scf.ec.gc.ca
While most of this site is useful to Bee Kids, click "Kid's Activities
and Education" for links to educational resources and games.
Presented in English and French!

GEOsources (the Canadian Geography Web site): www.ccge.org
Canada's top site to learn about its people and places. Offers quizzes.

National Atlas of Canada: www.atlas.gc.ca
Great technical information, maps, and educational materials.

California Geographical Survey World Atlas of Panoramic Images: www.humboldt.edu/~cga/ (click World Atlas)
Test your knowledge of mountains, rivers, peninsulas, and all the rest—from space! Accurate and downloadable, this perspective is very different from maps.

Google Earth: http://earth.google.com/
Curious about what La Paz, the Nile River, or the Fedchenko Glacier actually looks like from above? Google Earth takes you there. First, download the free software, then use the images to build your mental map of the world.

GREAT GEO GAMES
You'll find *GeoSpy, GeoBee Challenge* (also available as a board game), and lots of other National Geographic geography games at: http://kids.nationalgeographic.com/Games/GeographyGames

Carmen Sandiego. The Learning Company
This clever quiz game tests your geographic knowledge, from the USA and beyond.

Brain Quest—Know the States Game. Educational Insights, Rancho Dominguez, CA.

An entertaining board game that teaches locations, capital cities, American culture, and scenic features for all 50 states.

Name That Country Game. Educational Insights,
Rancho Dominguez, CA.
A board game that uses names, salutations, or special features on postcards to help you identify countries and capitals. The game can be played at varying levels of difficulty and tests knowledge of rivers, major cities, languages, and currencies.

Go Travel: Africa, South America. Travel by Games, Clinton, IA. These fun card games test your knowledge of history, geography, people, plants, animals, and problems on these continents.

GeoSafari Talking Globe. Educational Insights,
Rancho Dominguez, CA.
A talking geography quiz game and globe all in one. The 5,000-interactive-question database challenges players about their world knowledge. An advanced version offers 10,000 questions.

OTHER STUDY AIDS
Globes
Globes are available from a variety of manufacturers. Be sure to check the product date before ordering. Those produced by National Geographic can be found on the Society's Web site (www.nationalgeographic.com) or by calling 1-800-NGS-LINE .

Magazines

NATIONAL GEOGRAPHIC magazine, *National Geographic Kids*, *National Geographic Explorer, Canadian Geographic, Time for Kids* (TFK), and newsweeklies, such as *Time, Newsweek,* and *U.S. News & World Report*, include great articles, maps, graphs, and pictures.

Television

Programming on the National Geographic Channel, Public Television (*Nature, Bill Nye the Science Guy, Kratts' Creatures*, etc.), CNN, C-SPAN, the Discovery Channel, the History Channel, and nightly news broadcasts will greatly expand your world.

CD-ROMS:

The National Geographic Society, Rand McNally, GeoSafari, Hammond, and George F. Cram offer many digital versions of their world atlases, picture libraries, and other specific topics (history, world regions, exploration, etc.). Be sure to check the operating system requirements before purchasing any software.

Blank Outline Maps

Free downloads are available online from
National Geographic Xpeditions Atlas:
www.nationalgeographic.com/xpeditions/atlas
About Geography: http://geography.about.com/library/maps/blindex.htm
Arizona Geographic Alliance: http://alliance.la.asu.edu/azga/
Outline Maps of Canada: www.canadainfolink.ca/blankmap.htm
For a book of blank outline maps, contact the US Map and Book company (1-800-458-2306; www.usmapandbook.com).

Note to Teachers

The National Geographic Society developed the National Geographic Bee in response to concern about the lack of geographic knowledge among young people in the United States. In a ten-country Gallup survey conducted for the Society in 1988 and 1989, Americans 18 to 24 (the youngest group surveyed) scored lower than their counterparts in the other countries. Shocked by such poor results, the National Geographic Society spearheaded a campaign to return geography to American classrooms. Since 1989, the Bee has been one of several projects designed to encourage the teaching and study of geography. With nearly five million fourth through eighth graders entering each year, the Bee is one of the nation's most popular academic contests.

Some parents and even a few teachers think the Bee might resemble an orderly Trivial Pursuit contest. Yet, in more than a decade of coordinating the California State Bee, I have not seen a single adult who arrives with that opinion leave with it intact. Indeed, kids who correctly answer questions on topics such as glacial erosion, Hinduism, location, and changing political blocks humble a new flock of adults every year. The annual assembly of teachers, parents, and media is impressed not just with what the contestants know right off the bat, but also with how they methodically answer questions that at first appear to stump them. This ability to think like a geographer—to integrate physical, cultural, and economic knowledge—shines through at every level of the Bee.

Teaching young people to think like geographers provides them with vital understanding of the connections that exist between ourselves, our global neighbors, and the physical environment that supports us all. The U.S. Congress has recognized this important role by designating geography as one of ten core academic subjects included in federal education acts that have been passed into law since 1994. Unfortunately, geography in the No Child Left Behind Act that was passed in 2001 lacks the designated funding mandates that accompany other core academic subjects. Ongoing efforts by the National Geographic Society and others seek to improve this situation so that teachers can receive the support they need to provide crucial geographic education.

The National Geographic Society also offers many forms of support to teachers who seek to enhance the geographic education they provide to students. The national K–12 geography standards, published as *Geography for Life: National Geography Standards*, are a comprehensive presentation of what students should know and be able to do as the result of their educational experiences. Accompanying these voluntary national standards is *Path Toward World Literacy: A Standards Based Guide to K–12 Geography*, which presents a scope and sequence for teaching geography along with explanations and activities that assist teachers, curriculum writers, parents, and the general public to effectively integrate the geography standards into the school curriculum. The National Geography Standards have been incorporated into the curriculum frameworks of almost all of the 50 U.S. states.

In addition to the national K–12 geography standards, the National Geographic Society has established a Geography Alliance Network—university partnerships with local K–12 schools that has chapters in most U.S. states and provides training and support for educators. Whether teaching a stand-alone geography class or wishing to incorporate geography into other subjects such as history, science, or vocational education, teachers can tap into a wealth of resources through the Geographic Alliance Network. It offers opportunities for professional development training, ready-to-use lesson plans and other teaching resources, and interaction with a community of professionals at the local school, state, and university levels who provide the mentoring, contacts, assistance, and camaraderie that help to energize the daily task of teaching.

National Geographic also offers an education site and EdNet, an online community that provides education news, resources, discussion, and much more. Among the programs on EdNet, EarthCurrent News Digest contains links to bite-size news stories on classroom-perfect topics, such as archaeology and paleontology, exploration, peoples and cultures, plants and animals, science, and more. The education site provides links to maps, activities, and other programs for educators at National Geographic.

Contact information for schools to register for the Bee, obtaining the geography standards, locating a state Alliance, or obtaining online geography education information appears below. These are the perfect places to receive answers to your questions and to explore the world of possibilities in geography education.

Whether you are an experienced geo-educator or a newcomer, the Bee is a sure bet to stir student interest in the "Why of Where." Running the contest is simple. The Society provides registered schools with an instruction booklet, the questions and answers, certificates, and prizes. Think of the Bee as an open door to a world of fun and productive learning.

GEOGRAPHIC SUPPORT COORDINATES

To register for the National Geographic Bee

Principals of eligible U.S. schools can write to

National Geographic Bee

National Geographic Society

1145 17th Street N.W.

Washington, D.C. 20036-4688

Principals in U.S. schools with students in grades four through eight must register their schools to participate in the Bee by a deadline, usually October 15. Principals may request registration by writing on school letterhead and enclosing a check, purchase order, or money order for $90 (U.S. funds; cost in 2010) made payable to the National Geographic Society. For the most current information, call 202-828-6659 or go to the Bee Web site: nationalgeographic.com/geographicbee.

For information about the Canadian Geography Challenge go to

geochallenge.ca/geochallenge/register.asp

To find your state geographic alliance office and for other education resources, go to

nationalgeographic.com/education/

To order *Geography for Life: National Standards in Geography*, contact

store.ncge.net/merchant2

To order *Path Toward World Literacy*, contact

The Grosvenor Center for Geographic Education
Southwest Texas State University
601 University Drive
San Marcos, Texas 98666

www.geo.txstate.edu/grosvenor/publication.html

To order more copies of the third edition of *National Geographic Official Bee Study Guide* or *Afghanistan to Zimbabwe*, by 2004 Bee winner Andrew Wojtanik, go to any place books are sold or

www.ngchildrensbooks.com

Answers

Round 1
2. New Mexico
3. Montana
4. Kansas
5. Colorado River
6. Saguaro National Park
7. New York
8. South Carolina
9. Oregon
10. Hawai'i
11. Great Salt Lake
12. Oakland

Round 2
2. Los Angeles
3. Idaho
4. Maine
5. Illinois
6. Florida
7. Louisiana
8. Richmond
9. California

10. Texas
11. West Virginia
12. Oklahoma

Round 3
2. France
3. Namibia
4. Papua New Guinea
5. Thailand
6. Uzbekistan
7. Seychelles
8. Mexico
9. Romania
10. Botswana
11. France
12. Sweden

Round 4
2. South America
3. Egypt

4. Ireland
5. United Kingdom
6. Madagascar
7. Turkey
8. Philippines
9. Belgium
10. New Zealand
11. South Africa
12. Andes

Round 5
2. Europe
3. Africa
4. Antarctica
5. Australia
6. Asia
7. South America
8. Africa
9. Europe
10. Europe
11. Australia
12. North America

Round 6
2. meteorology
3. strait/channel
4. islands
5. geothermal energy
6. plate tectonics/continental drift
7. fjord
8. delta

9. epicenter
10. glacier/ice sheet
11. rain forest/selva
12. oasis

Round 7
2. Rhine River
3. India
4. Venezuela
5. Israel
6. Tanzania
7. Australia
8. United Kingdom/Great Britain/ Britain
9. Cyprus
10. Luxembourg
11. Côte d'Ivoire/Ivory Coast
12. Afghanistan

Tiebreaker Questions
2. Himalaya
3. California
4. San Marino
5. Tasmania
6. scale
7. Mandarin
8. Sri Lanka

Map Questions
1. New York
2. Kentucky
3. California
4. Georgia

5. Colorado
6. Nebraska
7. New Hampshire
8. South Carolina

2. 4
3. 2
4. 3
5. 4
6. 2
7. 1
8. 4
9. 4

Analogies
10. 3
11. 2
12. 4
13. 4

Graph Questions
15. 4
16. 1

STATE-LEVEL
Round 1
2. Denmark
3. Buenos Aires
4. Guatemala
5. Korea Peninsula
6. Bhutan

7. Sweden
8. India
9: Bogotá
10. Iceland

Round 2
2. frost action
3. atoll
4. Mediterranean
5. confluence
6. bedrock
7. jet stream
8. seismologist
9. monsoon
10. aquifer

Round 3
2. Austria
3. Suriname
4. Morocco
5. Pamirs
6. Luzon
7. Puerto Rico Trench
8. Ethiopia
9. Chad
10. Cambodia
11. Libya
12. Turkmenistan

Round 4
2. rice
3. Barcelona

4. North Sea
5. Bulgaria
6. France
7. Iran
8. Mexico
9. Cayman Islands
10. Kenya

Round 5
1. Iceland
2. Thailand
3. Norway
4. Fiji/Fiji Islands
5. Syria
6. Bangladesh
7. Kenya
8. Turkey
9. Bolivia
10. Denmark
11. Malaysia

Round 6
2. World War I
3. Jakarta
4. Valparaíso
5. Siberia
6. India
7. Bolivia
8. Thailand
9. Berlin
10. Tunisia
11. Ireland
12. Sudan

Round 7
2. Argentina, Chile
3. Laos
4. Portugal
5. South Africa
6. Spain
7. North Korea
8. Canada
9. Cuba
10. Gabon

Tiebreaker Questions
2. Suriname
3. Strait of Gibraltar
4. Baku
5. Sargasso Sea
6. Minsk
7. Morocco
8. Jamaica

Oral Analogies
1. Trinidad
2. Venezuela
3. Peru
4. Thailand
5. Canada
6. Czech Republic
7. Tanzania
8. Burkina Faso
9. Nepal
10. Denmark
11. Egypt
12. Sudan

Photo Questions
1. karst
2. Georgia
3. Chad
4. Tanzania

Map Questions
1. 5, Ashgabat
2. 16, Kobe
3. 11, Managua
4. 7, Casablanca
5. 22, Arequipa

NATIONAL LEVEL
Round 1
1. Baltic Sea
2. Pyrenees
3. Belize

Round 2
1. Cameroon
2. Jordan
3. Brazil

Round 3
1. Dublin
2. Greece
3. Ghana

Round 4
1. Belize City, Sydney, Kabul
2. China, Pakistan, Cambodia
3. Angola, Nigeria, Kenya

Round 5
1. arroyo
2. caldera
3. lagoon

Credits
p. 7, Brian Andreas's quote appears in *Geography,* by StoryPeople (www. storypeople.com); p. 11, Muhammad Ahmad Faris's quote appears in *The Home Planet,* conceived and edited by Kevin W. Kelly for the Association of Space Explorers, Addison-Wesley Publishing Company, New York, and Mir Publishers, Moscow; art p. 36, Shusei Nagaoka; p. 92 up, Bruce Dale, National Geographic Image Collection (NGIC); p. 92 low, George F. Mobley, NGIC; p. 93 up, Gordon Gahan, NGIC; p. 93 low, George F. Mobley, NGIC; front cover, Mark Thiessen, National Geographic; back cover: Mark Thiessen, National Geographic.

About the Author

Stephen F. Cunha is a professor of geography at California's Humboldt State University. He is also director of the California Geographic Alliance and state coordinator for the National Geographic Bee. He is the co-author of *Our Fifty States*, a children's reference book published by National Geographic. He and his family live near Redwood National Park.

Acknowledgments

Many talented people contributed to this book. Thanking Mary Hackett of the California Geographic Alliance for Russian around on our behalf requires a book in itself. I would have Ghana crazy without Mary Lee Elden, Megan Webster, Dan Malessa, Erin Dickinson, Geoffrey Hatchard, Tom Peyton, and Jo Erikson of the National Geographic Bee staff, who provided the questions. I would have Benin the dark about the Great Canadian Geography Challenge without Dale Gregory of Centennial School, British Columbia. Mary Cunha, geography lecturer at Humboldt State University, gave the entire manuscript a good Czech. The Bee kids who are the Seoul of Chapter 5 were totally cool. I also thank many young readers for sending me great suggestions—Ural great! Most important, I Congo on and on about Suzanne Patrick Fonda and Rebecca Baines of National Geographic Children's Books. Now that we are Finnish, I hope it makes you Hungary to learn Samoa geography!

Founded in 1888, the National Geographic Society is one of the largest nonprofit scientific and educational organizations in the world. It reaches more than 285 million people worldwide each month through its official journal, NATIONAL GEOGRAPHIC, and its four other magazines; the National Geographic Channel; television documentaries; radio programs; films; books; videos and DVDs; maps; and interactive media. National Geographic has funded more than 8,000 scientific research projects and supports an education program combating geographic illiteracy.

For more information, please call 1-800-NGS LINE (647-5463) or write to the following address:
National Geographic Society, 1145 17th Street N.W., Washington, D.C. 20036-4688 U.S.A.

Visit us online at www.nationalgeographic.com/books